Acclaim for *Portrait with Keys*

Winner of the South African *Sunday Times*
Alan Paton Non-Fiction Prize

Winner of the University of Johannesburg Prize

Longlist finalist for the Warwick Prize, UK

"*Portrait with Keys* knocked me out. It has Vladislavić's maverick take on the world and combines a warm and insightful view of Johannesburg with clever irony."
　　　　　　　　　　　　　　　　　—Zoe Wicomb

"If Italo Calvino had grown up in Jo'burg and experienced both apartheid and its aftermath, this is the kind of book he would have been proud to have written."
　　　　　　　　　　　　　　　　　—Geoff Dyer

"Jo'burg alarms and amazes. Guns, gold and sheer bloody glitz. For those, and you can count me in, who think it the greatest African city south of Cairo, Vladislavić has done us proud. He has celebrated the city in sharp and lovely images."
　　　　　　　　　　　　　　　　　—Christopher Hope

"Among the best South African literature in years. . . . There is a novelty to his very minting of language into image that matches the perpetual, compulsive 'start-from-scratch' ethos of Jo'burg that makes his book an instant, must-read classic."
　　　—Mark Gevisser, *The Sunday Independent* (Johannesburg)

"Vladislavić is a rare, brilliant writer. His work eschews all cant. Its sheer verve, the way it burrows beneath ossified forms of writing, its discipline and the distance it places between itself and the jaded preoccupations of local fiction, distinguish it."
　　　　　　　　　　　　　　　—*The Sunday Times* (Johannesburg)

D1016800

"Ivan Vladislavić writes of Johannesburg as a 'frontier city, a place of contested boundaries' where territory 'must be secured and defended or it will be lost'. But this isn't just a piece about alarmed houses and razor wire-topped fences. There's wildlife, together with violent poachers; and scenic waterways and lakes, only occasionally despoiled by bodies. It's a passionate account by a man who loves his city, shocking because it so embraces the things most people try to avoid thinking about. This collection has the crackle of authenticity about it."
—Tom Boncza-Tomaszewski, *The Independent on Sunday*

"Ivan Vladislavić has written a wonderful book about Johannesburg. For me it has been like reading an exceptionally perceptive reviewer on a play or a book I have loved, a reviewer who articulates brilliantly what I have only half perceived. . . . What Vladislavić's book has done is to touch minutely, sensuously, poetically, ironically and exactly on this strange, utilitarian town . . . and he has also recorded the astonishing variety of people whose lives have been transformed, not always happily, by the changes of the last fifteen years. This is a love letter to Johannesburg and a truly marvellous piece of work."
—Justin Cartwright, *Literary Review*

"[A] peculiar tension, between despair and delight, animates the city. In *Portrait with Keys*, Vladislavić unlocks it beautifully."
—Colin Murphy, *Irish Times*

"Vladislavić's acute intelligence and unfussy style make this quite a find."
—Jonathan Gibbs, *Metro*

"An outstanding writer and an intriguing subject."
—Sue Baker, *Publishing News*

"Vladislavić writes beautifully about the city he knows inside out, surveying the ways in which it has changed since the end of apartheid."
—Caroline Sanderson, *Bookseller*

Portrait with Keys

the city of Johannesburg unlocked

Ivan Vladislavić

W.W. Norton & Company
New York · London

For information about permission to reproduce selections from this book,
write to Permissions, W. W. Norton & Company, Inc.
500 Fifth Avenue, New York, NY 10110

For information about special discounts for bulk purchases, please contact
W. W. Norton Special Sales at specialsales@wwnorton.com or 800-233-4830

Manufacturing by Courier Westford
Book design by We Made This
Production manager: Devon Zahn

Library of Congress Cataloging-in-Publication Data

Vladislavic, Ivan, 1957–
Portrait with keys : the city of Johannesburg unlocked /
Ivan Vladislavic. — 1st American ed.
p. cm.
"Originally published in South Africa under the title
Portrait with keys : Joburg & what-what"—T.p. verso.
Includes bibliographical references.
ISBN 978-0-393-33540-8 (pbk.)
1. Johannesburg (South Africa)—Description and travel. 2. Johannesburg
(South Africa)—Social life and customs. 3. Johannesburg (South Africa)—Social
conditions. 4. Social change—South Africa—Johannesburg. 5. Vladislavic, Ivan,
1957– —Travel—South Africa—Johannesburg. 6. Vladislavic, Ivan, 1957– —
Homes and haunts—South Africa—Johannesburg. I. Title.
DT2405.J654V535 2009
968.22'106—dc22

2009005787

W. W. Norton & Company, Inc.
500 Fifth Avenue, New York, N.Y. 10110
www.wwnorton.com

W. W. Norton & Company Ltd.
Castle House, 75/76 Wells Street, London W1T 3QT

1 2 3 4 5 6 7 8 9 0

for
Tim Couzens

Memory takes root only half in the folds of the brain:
half's in the concrete streets we have lived along.

Lionel Abrahams

Contents

Point A

Haunted places are the only ones people can live in.
Michel de Certeau

When a house has been alarmed, it becomes explosive. It must
be armed and disarmed several times a day. When it is armed, by
the touching of keys upon a pad, it emits a whine that sends the
occupants rushing out, banging the door behind them. There
are no leisurely departures: there is no time for second thoughts,
for taking a scarf from the hook behind the door, for checking
that the answering machine is on, for a final look in the mirror
on the way through the hallway. There are no savoured home-
comings either: you do not unwind into such a house, kicking
off your shoes, breathing the familiar air. Every departure is pre-
cipitate, every arrival is a scraping-in.

In an alarmed house, you awake in the small hours to find
the room unnaturally light. The keys on the touch pad are aglow
with a luminous, clinical green, like a night light for a child
who's afraid of the dark.

How bad a man was Scrooge, that model of solitary mean-
spiritedness?

'Nobody ever stopped him in the street to say, with glad-
some looks, "My dear Scrooge, how are you? When will you
come to see me?" No beggars implored him to bestow a trifle,
no children asked him what it was o'clock, no man or woman
ever once in all his life inquired the way to such and such a
place, of Scrooge.'

The unequal exchange of directions is one of the most
touching relations possible between people in the city, and so it
is a measure of Scrooge's inhumanity that he was never once, in
all his life, engaged in it. Asking for directions, city people, who
set great store by their independence and hard-won knowledge
of the streets, who like to think that they 'know their way
around', declare their vulnerability; giving directions, they
demonstrate a capacity for dealing kindly and responsibly with a
life put in their hands by fate.

In the countryside it is different. Strangers and locals stand in a simpler relationship to one another. Strangers are few and far between, and they are therefore less threatening rather than more so, as one might suppose. Locals know the world around them like the backs of their hands, as the saying goes, and landmarks are more conspicuous and easier to describe. In any event, a country person (if he did not have the whim to send you on a wild goose chase) might think nothing of walking along with you, or driving ahead, to show you the way.

The busy city person must rely on words and gestures to guide the stranger through a clutter of irrelevant detail, with dead ends and false turns on every side, some of which might prove disastrous to the unwary. Giving directions is a singular skill, and doing so well a reliable measure of character. We need not be judgemental: the way we live in cities today, it is possible to lead a useful, happy life without learning the names of the streets in your own neighbourhood. It is also true that the complexity of cities, the flows of traffic across ever-changing grids, coupled with the peculiarities of physical addresses, occupations, interests and needs, produces for each one of us a particular pattern of familiar or habitual movement over the skin of the earth, which, if we could see it from a vantage point in the sky, would appear as unique as a fingerprint. It is literally impossible for certain of these paths to cross, which is why acquaintances may live in the same city, meeting by appointment as often as they choose, without ever running into one another in the daily round. But this is all the more reason why the crossing of paths, the places where they touch like wires in a circuit, for no better reason than chance, should be taken seriously.

When I was a child, my father, a city man through and through, a lover of walking and driving, finely attuned to change in the world around him and therefore able to give directions with creativity and precision, taught me that it never harmed anyone to have a map in hand. No lost soul was ever turned away from our door without a set of directions that would take him to his exact destination. We lived in a new suburb then, carved out of the veld on the outskirts of Pretoria; the world belonged to us, we were masters of all we surveyed. These were the days of the garden-variety wire fence, long before the advent of the candy-striped boom and the two-metre wall, when some stranger who had lost his way might hail a man mowing his lawn or tinkering with the engine of a car in the driveway. More often than not my dad would recognize the place at once and be able to give directions off the cuff. But even when he knew the way himself, he liked to send me or my brother Branko to fetch his map of the area, a detailed one acquired specially from the municipality, and spread it out on the bonnet of the stranger's car to point out the route. Perhaps the whole exercise was an excuse to have the stranger get out from behind the wheel and pass the time of day.

Since then, experience has taught me, and a host of writers have confirmed, that getting lost is not always a bad thing. One might even consider misdirecting a stranger for his own good.

I live just around the corner from the Marymount Nursing 3 Home. In fact, I often use it as a landmark when giving people directions to my door. In the winter months, when you can see through the naked branches of the oaks in the dead end of Blenheim Street, the building announces itself in large white letters on orange brick. In summer it all but disappears behind the foliage.

Several times over the years it has happened that a guest in my home, leaning on the parapet of the stoep with a cup of tea and looking out over the treetops into the valley, has suddenly recognized the building jutting out on the ridge, and exclaimed: 'Is that the Marymount? I was born there!' A silence always falls after this unexpectedly intimate revelation, while the spirit of place casts a spell over our hearts. But it only lasts a moment, for there is something about the marmalade-brick building, with its white plaster and corrugated-iron roof, that prevents us from thinking too deeply about our origins.

I used to consider it a remarkable coincidence that so many people in my circle should have had their beginnings within a stone's throw of my house. But my brother Branko, who is more of a realist than I am, boiled it down to statistical probabilities. In the fifty years of the Marymount's operation, more than two hundred thousand babies came into the world within its walls. Ten or eleven babies a week, on average, with peaks around September. You can hardly turn a corner in Johannesburg without bumping into a Marymount baby.

Branko also took the mystery out of why I was always being called upon to direct anxious parents-to-be towards the nursing home, a service I performed half a dozen times in as many years. 'It stands to reason,' he said, 'that anyone following the sign from Kitchener Avenue will lose their way on the corner of Blenheim and Argyle. It's the first unmarked intersection, the first point at which they have to make a decision for themselves. And seeing that your house is right there, and that you must go in and out through the front gate every day, someone casting about for directions is bound to seize upon you from time to time. It's the law of averages.'

Although I cannot claim to have chosen my house on the strength of its proximity to the Marymount, like some peasant eager to live in the shadow of the church or within walking distance of the well, its presence was always reassuring (I would never admit this to my brother): every week, a flock of new human souls came into the world on my doorstep. And so it is a pity that the home has closed down. The last baby was born there in June 1997. The number of births had been tapering off for years, as more and more white doctors moved further north, taking their patients with them. People in the northern suburbs no longer believe that a decent person would want to be born on this side of town.

It was a year before posters went up in the neighbourhood advertising the public auction of the property. Two groups with very different plans for the place made bids for ownership: a consortium of midwives and doctors intended to revive it as a nursing home; a consortium of businessmen proposed to transform it into low-cost housing or a park for light industry. Dry-cleaners and panel beaters. New lives of a different sort. But neither group has been able to raise the finance.

Hurrying home, half my mind on the work I've just delivered to a client in Doris Street, the other half on the soccer. South Africa is playing Denmark in the first round of the 1998 World Cup and I'm supposed to meet my brother Branko at the Ab Fab to watch the game. I don't want to miss the kick-off. Suddenly it's as if a lasso tightens around my ankles. I've got one hand in my pocket, the other hooked by the thumb into the strap of my rucksack, so I can't even put out a hand to break my fall. I go down full-length, just managing a slight twist to avoid falling on my face. There's an almighty crack somewhere below my jaw, like a bone breaking. I lie there dazed and winded for a moment. My feet seem to be tied together. Am I being mugged? I have an impression of people nearby, so I play possum. No, it's just me here on the pavement in Roberts Avenue. I roll over and sit up. There is a loop of thick white paper around my ankles. I try to break it but it holds, and I have to slide it down over my shoes and squirm out of it. One seamless piece, barely large enough for my feet to fit through. How on earth did this happen?

Just beside me is the palisaded boundary wall of the medical suites at the Kensington Clinic. Useful. A security guard is sitting there, on the edge of his seat, looking at me through the bars with a worried face. 'Haai shame,' he says. On the other side, on the grass verge of the street, another worried face, a woman, a hawker. The two of them were talking as I came up. He was slouching in a garden chair, she was sitting behind her counter, a pine plank balanced across a cardboard box, displaying a few oranges and apples, half a box of cigarettes, little plastic bags full of peanuts and Chappies bubblegum. I have fallen like a drunkard over the guy-ropes of their conversation, jerking them both towards me.

She comes closer. If we were different people, if we were the same people in a different place, she might put an arm around my shoulders; instead she lifts her hand and drops it a couple of times, meaningfully, and clucks sympathetically. Something wet is running down my side. Am I bleeding? I feel around inside my jacket. Red wine, seeping out of the rucksack. The crack was a bottle breaking, my thank-you present from the people in Doris Street. I am leaking nothing more essential than merlot.

The usual adult embarrassment at falling down overwhelms me. I assure the guard that I am fine, I even show him the paper loop with an incredulous laugh. Then I get to my feet, dust off my knees and hurry on, leaving a bloody trail of wine. As soon as I'm out of view of the witnesses, I begin to limp. For some reason, I appear to be putting this limp on a bit, exaggerating, as the physical expression of feeling sorry for myself. Haai shame, my limp says to me, you've had a fall. A damp patch of wine spreads down my side. I must smell like a tramp. When I look for my keys at the door, I realize that the white strip is dangling from my hand like an unravelled bandage.

Aching too much to watch the soccer, and annoyed with myself, I take a hot bath and go to bed. The game ends in a draw.

The next day, my right arm is so bruised and painful that I cannot work. I sit at my desk and examine the loop under the reading light. It seems to be a piece of packaging, an innocuous oval, about twenty centimetres across. Somehow, I must have stood on one end, stepped in the other… it looks so improbable. The feeling that I have been the victim of a practical joke will not leave me. I drop the loop on the carpet and it lies there like a snare. Stand on the near end with the tip of my left slipper, slide the toe of my right slipper under the far end. Now for the left. Never mind improbable, it seems impossible. But standing on the thing reawakens the sensation of falling and makes my shoulder ache.

When I pick the loop up again, I realize for the first time that it has a twist in it. It is a Möbius strip. A one-sided figure, a three-dimensional object with only one surface. I have fallen over a paradox. This thought makes me feel better. I put my pen gingerly on the loop and run it along the surface, like a child guiding a hoop with a stick, and after a while I arrive back at the starting point.

I live on an island, an accidental island, made by geography and the town planners who laid out these city streets. Roberts and Kitchener, avenues in the uniforms of English soldiers, march away to the east, side by side. A spine of rock, an outcrop of the gold-bearing reef on which the city depends, blocks every thoroughfare between the avenues, except for Blenheim and Juno. When I am driven to walk, which is often, only the long way round, following this shore – Blenheim, Roberts, Juno, Kitchener – will bring me back to the beginning. Johannesburg surges and recedes like a tide. I come home with my shoes full of sand, empty my pockets at the kitchen table and pick through the findings. The roar in the air is the absence of water.

My friend Paul had a house on the cliff in Bellevue Street. As we leant on the parapet one night, looking out over the rooftops of Bez Valley, with the lights twinkling in the distance on Yeoville ridge like beacons on a headland, he said that it would be a fine thing if they built a dam and filled this valley up with water, drowned every house and factory, every aerial and chimney. Then he would have an ocean to complement his ocean view. If you closed your eyes, the traffic on Kitchener Avenue in the valley below, a rubbery squish of tyres on tar, sounded very much like surf.

For a moment the shell of the city was pressed to my ear.

Johannesburg, as people often remark, is one of the few major cities in the world that has no river, lake or ocean. It has a reef, of course, but no diving.

I walk, in the afternoons, along something as unnatural and persuasive as an extended metaphor.

6   A few days after the auction of the Marymount, the cobbler who has set up shop on the corner of Nourse and Hillier Streets was putting one of the posters to good use by spreading his tools out on it. The neighbourhood's first street-corner hawker. He has chosen an auspicious location, opposite the neighbourhood's national monument: the house where Mahatma Gandhi lived in the first decades of the century. You can see the little plaque from the National Monuments Council on the west-facing wall as you come down Nourse Street. The house is a double-storey on a promontory between Hillier and Albemarle Streets, with a beautiful panel of stained-glass sunshine to light the stairs and a second-storey balcony like the rounded prow of a riverboat.

For a while, the people who live in the Gandhi House, as we call it around here, kept a tree in their garden made entirely of metal, no doubt highly resistant to drought, with fanciful, curly branches like a candelabrum, where a cast-iron owl was perched. But it is gone now, dead of rust or carried away in the night by a scrap-metal dealer.

7   When my car, a white Ford Meteor with eighty thousand kilometres on the clock, was stolen from outside my house, I immediately phoned my father. He listened sympathetically. Then he asked: 'Did you ever get yourself a Gorilla?'

He had been pestering me for months to buy a steering lock, and I had been putting it off. Now the car was gone. I was on the point of lying: Yes, Dad, I got myself a Gorilla, just as you suggested, but the thieves cut it off with an angle grinder. Went through it like butter. But you cannot deceive my father about such things. 'No,' I said sheepishly. 'I meant to, I really did. But for one reason or another I never got round to it.'

'That's a pity.' There was a long, crackling silence. 'You know, the guys who make the Gorilla are so confident about their product, they offer the purchaser a special guarantee: if your car gets stolen with the Gorilla in place, they'll refund half the excess on your insurance. Ah well, once bitten, twice shy. Perhaps you'll be more careful next time.'

The town planners who defined the boundary between Troyeville and Kensington did not follow the suggestion of a street, which seems to be the norm; instead they drew a line behind the houses on the western side of Albemarle Street, where the back walls of the plots adjoin those of the houses behind them. Rather than meeting face to face, the two suburbs turn their backs on one another.

The recent history of the house at 22 Albemarle Street, strictly in Kensington, is nonetheless typical of the frontier suburb which Troyeville has become, a contested zone between inner-city suburbs like Fairview and New Doornfontein, which have evolved into black areas, and Kensington, which still holds on to its white identity.

The house is a renovation of the kind found in suburbs with a large Portuguese population (Troyeville and Bez Valley in the east, say, or Rosettenville and La Rochelle in the south). In a standard Portuguese renovation the structure is squared off, the fat pillars that once held up the verandah roof are replaced with angular, painted piping and the stoep and pathways are tiled; in more extreme versions, the entire facade may be tiled and the garden cemented over, with the occasional porthole provided for a scrawny rosebush to stick out its neck. In the Albemarle Street house, there is a low garden wall of brick topped with wrought-iron curlicues, a tiled path bisecting two squares of lawn, leading to glass doors in a rounded archway. The verandah has been closed in and provided with four lancet-arch windows, in pairs on either side of the doors. These windows are outlined in narrow panels of frosted, bottle-brown glass. Across the top of the flat facade is a single row of mosaic tiles – or it may be some kind of veneer – stuck to the guttering.

The house was put up for sale in 1997. Perhaps the owner was frightened off when the old lady at 17 Blenheim Street was murdered. The murderers, surprised in the act by a neighbour, jumped over the back wall into the yard of the house behind, just a few doors up from No. 22, and escaped into Albemarle Street. After several months on the market and a string of show days, there were still no buyers, and for a time the house stood empty. Finally, it was put up for rent.

The first black tenants moved in. It was around then that a sticker bearing the slogan of the anti-crime campaign – I DON'T DO CRIME – appeared on the glass door: either an appeal to the better nature of prospective burglars or an attempt by the new tenants (or their landlord) to reassure the neighbours.

For a while the new tenants stayed indoors. Then, as they grew more comfortable in the area, they became more visible. Soon there were children pushing toy cars on the path or playing soccer in the street. Tricycles and dolls lay on the lawn. Men lounged about on the steps or worked on cars at the kerbside, and women sat on upturned oildrums, catching the sun on a wintry afternoon.

'What's wrong with these people?' my brother Branko said during one of our walking tours. 'Why don't they stay inside like normal people? Why are they always lazing about in the yard? Have they got nothing better to do with their time than sit around in the sun?'

'But you're the one who's always complaining that there's no life on the streets,' I said, 'and how terrible it is that people feel trapped in their own homes. Just last week you were remembering how we used to play cricket under the street lights at night after supper, when we were kids.'

'What's with the paint tins?' he said grumpily. 'Can't they get proper garden furniture? You can pick up a plastic chair for twenty bucks at Dion's.'

A few weeks later, Branko was insisting the place had been turned into a brothel. On his way down to see me one morning, he noticed a woman sitting on the kerb outside, with a towel draped over her shoulders that said AMBASSADOR HOTEL. She was separating the strands of her thick braids so that they would dry in the sun, her fingers moving over her scalp as if she was working the fibres of some plant into matting. He slowed down to get a good look at her, he said, and she gave him a sly smile.

A brothel? It seemed possible. But the very next Sunday, as I was walking to the shops to fetch the paper, a black churchman, like a biblical prophet in his white cotton robes, came out of the house and made his way up the hill to Roberts Avenue ahead of me. He carried a stick carved into a cross, and a Bible with golden edges stuck out of a pocket in his tunic. In the small of his back, stitched to a broad red cummerbund, was a pure blue circle the size of a coaster.

Where would his congregation meet? In a clearing in the veld near the municipal dump in Elandsfontein; in a sealed room under the motorway in Newtown, filled with pitted wooden benches and the incense of exhaust fumes; beneath a tree on Langermann Kop?

As he walked he patted his hair with the palm of his hand, and looked at the shadow of his head on the ground. Involuntarily I smoothed my own hair by combing it through with my fingers, and was reminded that we live differently in our bodies and our houses. But I had resolved not to pursue such difficult and divisive lines of thought, especially over weekends, and so I veered into Tile City in Op de Bergen Street for a chat with the hardware man.

The house at 18 Eleanor Street is another Portuguese modern- 9
ization, but more restrained. It once had three notable features,

all of them amulets against danger, but only one has survived. In the left-hand corner of the severely cropped lawn sat a life-size statue of a German shepherd dog, with painted fur and a grinning jaw. It looked like a large-scale version of the SPCA collection boxes that used to stand on shop counters. On the right-hand facade of the house, the second and third amulets were arranged symmetrically on either side of the central window (a bedroom, to judge by lacy curtains behind Spanish bars), like icons at an altar. On the left, a rectangular panel composed of six blue ceramic tiles, together depicting the Virgin Mary; on the right, a signboard, of exactly the same size and colour, declaring that the house was protected by the N.I.S.S. armed response company.

This house has been sold to a coloured family, who apparently have no taste for Roman Catholic iconography. After tolerating her presence for a few months, they chiselled the Madonna of Eleanor Street off the wall, leaving behind a patch of white plaster as clear as a conscience in the cream-coloured paintwork. Or was it the previous owner who came back to fetch her? The dog is gone too, but the N.I.S.S. sign endures.

The spot where David Webster was shot dead by an apartheid assassin is just across the road.

10   Not long after Minky and I came to live in Blenheim Street, new people moved into the house at No. 10. And not long after that, they employed a woman to paint a Ndebele design on their garden wall. As I was passing by one morning, I saw her marking out the pattern with a felt-tip pen on the white surface, and over the following days I went up the road regularly to watch her progress. When she had finished the pattern, an immense maze of black lines, six or seven metres long and two metres high, she began to fill it in with paint – mainly blue and green, if memory serves me correctly. She used little tins of Plascon, the standard household enamel, and ordinary brushes of the kind

you can buy at the hardware store.

There was a fad for Ndebele painting at the time. A woman called Esther Mahlangu had been commissioned to coat a BMW 525 in Ndebele colours as part of an advertising campaign. Or was it an art project? Either way, it was a striking symbolic moment in the invention of the new South Africa, a supposedly traditional, indigenous culture laying claim to one of the most desirable products our consumer society had to offer, smoothly wrapping this contemporary symbol of status, wealth and sophisticated style in its colours. Perhaps this same woman had wound up here in Kensington? No, I decided, Mahlangu's saloon had been seen all around the world, she had made a name for herself. She would surely have moved on to commissions larger and grander than garden walls – churches, convention centres, hotel dining rooms, the lobbies of health and racquet clubs.

My friend Liz said the whole Ndebele fad was kitsch. 'It's like that braai sauce people slosh over everything to give it an African flavour. Tomatoes and onions and too much chilli. Someone just made it up.'

'But that's how culture evolves,' I said. 'People make things up. Who's to say what will be regarded as "authentic" a generation from now? Why shouldn't we have Ndebele patterns on suburban walls? What if the people living there happen to be Ndebele? Anyway, only someone with a custodial view of African culture would regard as "traditional" an art form that arose so recently. Ndebele wall painting is no more than a few decades old, it's constantly changing, and it's full of contemporary references.' We were standing on the pavement outside No. 10 as we spoke, and so I could refer to the bright new mural in support of my point. 'This funnel shape here, which looks like a geometric abstraction, is actually a stylized light. One of those cheap industrial light-shades you'd see in a factory or a servant's room. Once you know that, you'll realize that the little dab of yellow at the bottom is a lightbulb. Charming, don't you think? And this shape here, which looks like a bow tie, is derived from a sweet. A boiled sweet in a plastic wrapper.'

Liz was impressed with my analysis (which I'd found in a magazine article about Esther Mahlangu, to tell the truth), but sceptical about the mural. 'It's so cheerful,' she said, 'it makes me want to spit. Like a kiddie's colouring book, with nothing outside the lines. That's why you whites like it so much. Nice and tidy.'

I thought it was bravely optimistic. It suited the early nineties perfectly: Africa was coming to the suburbs in the nicest possible way. I grew to love that wall. My only fear was that some racist would deface it. I could already see the insulting graffiti, dripping bile. But no one ever laid a finger on it.

Long afterwards, it occurred to me that I might have documented the making of the mural. It would have made a wonderful photographic essay. Or even better, a film. That intricate pattern, vibrant and complex as stained glass – it was no child's drawing, never mind what Liz said – spreading out, segment by segment, over a blank white wall. What a metaphor for the social transformation we were living through!

'If only you were a film-maker,' Minky said, 'or a photographer.'

'But I'm a writer, for Pete's sake, I could have spoken to the painter. I should have got her name, at least. I'm walking around with my eyes wide open, taking everything in like a vacuum cleaner, coughing bits of it out on paper. But I never bother to get the facts.'

11 The father of one of my high-school classmates was a part-time inventor, and his brightest idea was the telephone dixie, a little desk-top cabinet for the tidy and convenient storage of telephone directories. The open-fronted box held three heavy-duty ledger files, hinged at the bottom so that they could be tilted out and opened flat. Using a simple mechanism of springy clasps, you could secure in these files the Yellow Pages and two directo-

ries of your choice – let's say Johannesburg and the West Rand – and they were guaranteed to stay spick and span through a year of regular use. It was a fine and necessary invention. There was an executive model, as I recall, in lightly padded vinyl, but even the plain metallic models were superbly made. I have forgotten the exact finishes, but the colour schemes of the day were culinary: mustard, burgundy, cream.

The school holidays came, and my friend and I were engaged as salesmen. For my friend, who lived in what is now Midrand, then known with more charm as Halfway House, 'town' was not Pretoria, as it was for me, but Johannesburg, and it was to that thrillingly unfamiliar city we went to do business. Every morning for a week, I tramped through the endless corridors of the Carlton Centre, in my school flannels and my father's tie, hawking the telephone dixie.

It was 1972 and the Carlton Centre had just been built. An enormous complex of offices and shops, with a total floor area of 3.5 million square feet, of which 1.9 million square feet were below street level. Colour scheme: orange. You could smell the paint on the walls and the latex adhesive on the wall-to-wall carpets. There was an air of supreme sophistication about the entire complex. One index of this was the colour-coded maps on shiny boards, showing the different blocks and shopping levels, and the numbers of individual shops; and alongside the boards an information booth, where a uniformed official sat ready to offer guidance if you lost your way. Surely such elaborate precautions had never been required before *inside* a building? They confirmed the vast and labyrinthine dimensions of the place.

Then I had not yet read Frank Bettger's *How I Raised Myself from Failure to Success in Selling*, which Dale Carnegie himself adjudged the most helpful and inspiring book on salesmanship he had ever read, and so my expertise was slight. My friend fared little better. But despite our evident lack of success, we laboured steadily up the floors of the office tower, my friend plying the even numbers and I plying the odd, demonstrating the virtues of the telephone dixie to anyone who would listen, and praying for orders. Our rise to the top took several days. Often I got no further than the receptionists, who sometimes made me wrestle with the spring-loaded clips for their own amusement. Occasionally I made it into the offices of junior managers and senior clerks. Here, with the whole city for a backdrop, every white person capable of sitting up straight behind a desk appeared to be a business magnate. Up we went, floor by floor. The higher we toiled, the more spectacular the views became. On a clear day, it was said, you could see Pretoria. I began to relish the moments when the person whose precious time I was wasting would leave the room to attend to more pressing concerns, so that I could stand before the window and look down at the immensity of the city, assured that even a hawker of telephone dixies could occupy the centre of it all. It was in those reflective moments that my sense of the unnatural beauty of Johannesburg was born and that I resolved to seek my fortune in these streets.

At the end of a busy morning, the sales team had lunch at the Pumpernickel on Level 200. The food was unlike anything we had ever seen. There were frankfurters with notches carved into their convex curves and skinny potato chips with corrugated edges. There were bangers wrapped in bacon and dribbled with melted cheese, all held together with toothpicks. The fruit juices had little umbrellas unfurled in them; the paper sleeves of the drinking straws had been teased into decorative ruffs. While we scoffed the only material rewards of our efforts, the demonstration dixies stood at heel beside our chairs like well-trained dogs.

12   Every month for the past fifteen years, on the second Thursday of the month to be precise, I have met my brother Branko for coffee at the Carlton Centre (to which he is also sentimentally attached, for reasons of his own). I could chart the life and death

of this great complex by the sequence of coffee shops which came to serve as our regular meeting place over the years: from the Koffehuis, where the waitresses were got up as Dutch dairy-maids in clogs and lace caps, to the Brazilian Coffee Bar, where the cups and saucers arrived and departed on a conveyor belt.

When we first began meeting, the parkade in Main Street, opposite the hotel, was always full. You would have to wind up the spiral ramp to the fourth or fifth floor to find a bay. Little arrows and neon signs saying FULL and UP, in red and green respectively, kept you circling higher until a floor would accept you. There were attendants too, the obligatory middlemen between motorists and machinery, waving you on. The shiny concrete gave unexpected squeals of delight beneath the tyres. When you finally came to rest, you had to memorize the colour of the floor and the number of the bay or you would never find your way back. There were four lifts, large enough to park a Volkswagen in. Even here, in the parkade, the slightly unsettling smell of food, which came to circulate in the atmosphere of the entire centre once the paint fumes had worn off, reminded you that pleasurable consumption lay ahead.

Then, in the mid-nineties, the parkade began to shrink. The demand for parking fell, level by level, like a barometer of change in the city centre. The people with cars were clearly going elsewhere. You could find parking on the fourth floor now, and after a while on the third, and then always on the second or first. Finally the illuminated arrows were switched off.

In May 1998 – it would have been Thursday the 14th – when I turned into Main Street, there was a chain slung across my usual entrance. The middleman, who had always been there at the boom to catch the ticket the machine spat out and hand it to me through the window, was nowhere to be seen. Instead a sign urged me down an unfamiliar ramp into the basement. A long tunnel, with odd twists and turns in it, peculiar level land-ings and sudden lurching descents, took me down below the ground. I soon lost my sense of direction. Eventually I found myself in a crowded corner of the basement, where the cars were all huddled like refugees. An armed guard oversaw my arrival. I made my way to the nearest lift, but there was a label pasted across the crack between the doors, as if to prevent them from opening: HOTEL CLOSED. It reminded me of a crime scene in an American TV series. The guard appeared at my shoulder and directed me to a distant lift, which brought me out in an unpopulated alley of the centre, an area I had last ventured into with a telephone dixie in my hand.

As we sat drinking our espressos at the little counter in the office block, which has the knack of making you feel like you're in New York, my brother told me that he couldn't face the city any more. It's too dangerous, he said, and unpleasant anyway, what with empty shops and echoing corridors and the smell of piss in the doorways. We should move our monthly meetings to Rosebank or Illovo. There are coffee shops in the suburbs where you can still read your paper and eat your biscotti in peace. What about Eastgate?

When I resurfaced into the chilly air a little later, a fierce white light caught my eye. Welders in overalls were sealing off the canopied entrance to the Carlton Hotel behind a palisade fence.

13   Sophie Calle's exhibition *The Detachment/Die Entfernung* is on at the Johannesburg Art Gallery in Joubert Park. She describes her way of working: 'I visited places from which symbols of the former East Germany have been effaced. I asked passers-by to describe the objects that once filled these empty spaces. I photographed the absence and replaced the missing monuments with their memories.' The photographs show empty niches, overturned pedestals, unscrewed plaques. In the accompanying texts, the citizens of East Berlin recollect the displaced memorials as best they can, accurately or not, with or without fondness; there are also photographs of the old times, when the symbols of power still occupied their places with confidence, and these

allow us to stand in judgement on the veracity of the recorded memories.

A bell rings to signal that the gallery is about to close. I stop at the toilet in the basement on the way out. A street child, as filthy as a chimney sweep, comes out of one of the cubicles with a length of toilet paper dangling from his pocket and starts to wash his face at a basin. While I'm wringing my hands under the dryer, a security guard bursts in, grabs the boy by his arm, and hustles him away.

I go out into the deserted gallery. On my left, set into the curved wall that discreetly screens the toilets from the exhibition space, is a concrete ledge, and happening to glance down as I pass it, I see a grubby white sneaker sticking out. I bend down and look under the ledge. There is an oddly shaped recess I would never have noticed. Two small boys are crammed into it. They smell of wood smoke and sweat. They draw in their legs and look at me with big eyes. What should I do? Should I tell the security guard? Or should I let them have a warm bed for the night? Like a true art lover, I go on my way ambivalently, turning the options over in my mind. I pass through the empty halls, past African crafts and nineteenth-century oils, I go down the steps into the parking lot, and the guard locks the door behind me.

Chas is going to live in Cape Town at the end of the year. For some months, ever since Branko abandoned me, I have been accompanying my friend on his goodbye walks, revisiting, recalling and relinquishing the parts of Joburg he expects to miss despite himself. The city, we agree, is no more than a mnemonic. Where do we go? Here and there. What do we talk about? This and that. What do we see?

In July, for instance, as we made our way along Empire Road through the S-bend at Helpmekaar Hoërskool, we discovered, atop a wall on the left, an innovative anti-scaling device known

14

as 'Hercules Cacti'. Stepping gingerly through tangled ivy, and assuring ourselves first that the device was not electrified, we examined it in detail. 'Hercules Cacti' consisted of cylindrical segments, fiercely spiked and barbed all round with outgrowths like pineapple tops, apparently of metal but coated for durability, mounted horizontally on long axles fixed to the top of the wall. Ingenious, we said to one another, spinning a segment and watching it whirr. The thief hasn't been born who could get over here. More expensive than spikes, undoubtedly, but twice as effective. Probably more expensive than electric fencing too, but then there would be no running costs or maintenance. Looks indestructible. And quite natural, almost like thorn branches, especially in that olive drab. Then we backed away to the pavement, dusted the turn-ups of our trousers, and went on.

15 Further discoveries awaited us in Pieter Roos Park, where Victoria and Empire meet. In the south-western corner, the remains of a primitive outdoor gymnasium, from the heyday of jogging and Jane Fonda, with apparatus made of wooden posts for jumping over and hoisting oneself up on, all quite unfit for use. In the north-eastern corner, a metal sculpture, vaguely suggestive of a prehistoric bird, with two black men asleep in the shade of its belly. One opened an eye and glared at us balefully. The only other white men in the park appeared to be tramps.

In the middle, a grove of bluegums. The scent of eucalyptus reminded Chas of his boyhood home in Vereeniging, and that he is saying goodbye not just to Joburg but to the Transvaal, which no longer exists, to the Highveld, to the interior.

Then I too was reminded of my childhood, in a new suburb laid out in the veld on the edge of Pretoria. The houses were new and in the American style, or so we thought, with their big glass windows and garages attached to one end; and the roads were long, straight and newly tarred, and fragrant with cow dung. In the mornings the herdboys would drive the cattle along Von Willich Avenue to graze in the veld on the edge of the suburb, and in the evenings they would bring them back again to the whitewashed stalls of the smallholdings, where the bluegums shed long smooth curls of bark on which it was possible to write the life story of a marooned man. Electricity pylons marched to the east and west across the veld, and the Voortrekker Monument squatted on the distant horizon.

On a midwinter morning in 1997, a householder in the suburb of Saxonwold surprised an armed man trying to break into his home and raised the alarm. The burglar fled along Jan Smuts Avenue with the police in pursuit and took refuge in the grounds of the Zoo. When he was cornered, he jumped over a wall into an enclosure that happened to house Max, the Zoo's 180 kilogram gorilla. Perceiving his partner Lisa to be under threat, Max grabbed hold of the robber and bit him, whereupon the man fired three shots from a .38 special, hitting Max in the shoulder and neck. The police, who had gathered on the viewing platform, returned fire, hitting the suspect in the groin.

Four policemen and two zookeepers then entered the night enclosure in an effort to evacuate the wounded man. Sergeant Percy Alberts managed to handcuff him – he was still full of fight – but as he and his men were withdrawing, the enraged gorilla attacked them. He threw Constable Amos Simelane on the ground and roughed him up a bit. Then he seized Constable Robert Tshabalala and bit him on the upper arm and buttocks. Finally, he dislocated Sergeant 'Rassie' Rasenele's arm. At this point one of the zookeepers managed to drive Max off by turning a fire extinguisher on him, and the men made good their escape.

The injured policemen and the suspect were taken to the Garden City Clinic. The Zoo's own veterinarians sedated Max and tried to treat him on the spot, but their X-ray equipment proved inadequate for the bulky frame of a Western Lowland gorilla and so he was conveyed under police escort to the Milpark Hospital. 'There were emotional scenes as the unconscious primate was gently placed on the back of the bakkie,' one paper reported. Indeed, there was an outpouring of tender concern from all quarters. Pictures showed Max lying on a stretcher under a blanket, with his head thrown back and his teeth bared, while a veterinarian tended to a drip. Another burly vet cradled Max's head, the fingers of one hand shielding his eyes, the others cupped under his chin. Perhaps it was this man who held Max's hand during the surgery to locate and remove the bullets. Some of Johannesburg's finest surgeons assisted in the procedure at no cost. On the admission form, Max's profession was given as 'Gorilla', his employer as the Johannesburg Zoo.

17   There are three approaches to the Gem Supermarket on the corner of Roberts Avenue and Blenheim Street: steps rise from the pavement to the door in the middle of the facade, and two L-shaped ramps slope up to the same point from left and right. On either side of the steps, each ramp encloses a space like a stall, edged by a low wall and a metal railing behind, and open to the pavement in front.

In the right-hand stall a cobbler has set up shop. He has a plastic milk crate for a workbench and an empty paint tin for a stool. His blades, awls and files are laid out on a strip of cloth. After he packs up in the afternoon and goes home, black crosses and arrows, sprinklings of rubber filings from the past day's work, which have stencilled the corners of boxes and crates on the cement paving, still mark the space as his.

The focal point of the cobbler's stall is a collection of old shoes waiting to be repaired, or already repaired and offered for sale. They're usually displayed in a cardboard box, but sometimes he sets them out in a long row of pairs, one on top of the other. Most of them are worn-out and misshapen, with the uppers caved in and the toes turned up, the unlaced vamps folded over one another like the cuffs of a corpse. When you prise them open, you find the X-ray outlines of toes, heels, the balls of the feet on the insoles. You cannot help thinking that the people who wore these shoes are dead now. Even when they've been resoled and restitched, and given a coat of polish, just looking at them is enough to make your feet sore.

All day, the cobbler bows over his work. Sometimes he jokes quietly with the kids waiting for the bus or chats over his shoulder with the Gem's security guard, who has a chair in the shade on the ramp behind him, but his hands keep busy, kneading the unyielding leather, punching through it with an awl, pushing a long needle into the holes.

A young white man with a bristly face and yellow hair has occupied the other stall. He is strong and energetic, but even in the summer he appears to be cold. He wears thick, checked shirts and scarves, and his skin is pink and drawn. He paces up and down in the narrow stall, four paces to the right, and a clockwise turn, four paces to the left, and an anticlockwise turn, up and down for hours on end, looking at his feet. Sometimes he swings his arms, beating them against his sides as if he's freezing, trying to keep the circulation going. His pacing is hypnotic, up and down in front of the railing, like a caged animal. The fact that the cage has no bars on one side, that he could simply walk out of it if he chose, makes his ceaseless pacing more compelling. People stop to stare at him, especially children. When they realize that he is oblivious they sometimes go close and examine him, as if there really were bars between them to authorize an intimate scrutiny.

I stare at him myself, more discreetly. He lives in the boarding house on the other side of the intersection, according to Mannie the pawnbroker. That's where you'll find him when he's not here outside the Gem. I want to see him stop, pick up the rucksack that's lying in one corner and go across the street. I want to see him step out of the cage. But I always grow tired of watching before he is tired of pacing.

Four strides, a clockwise turn, four strides, an anticlockwise turn. It would be better if both were clockwise: then one might console oneself that he is accumulating distance. As it is, these turns in opposite directions cancel out progress, create the impression that he is constantly retracing his steps, always forgetting why he is moving and going back to the starting point. He is going nowhere, fast. He has a bitter set to his mouth, a muscle throbbing in his jaw.

Although I have seen the cobbler and the caged man in their places many times, it is months before the two scenes fold together like the wings of an icon: the black man quietly working, with the pile of old shoes beside him, and the white man restlessly pacing. Both with their heads bowed, both intent on what they are doing. A connection crackles between them that will not easily be broken. They are figures in a parable. The caged man is wearing out shoes as fast as the cobbler can mend them. But where does it start? Which panel of the diptych should we favour? Is the caged man making the cobbler work? Or is the cobbler making the caged man walk?

18   I parked my car in Prospect Road and headed into Hillbrow. It was winter, night was falling early and it felt like the millennium fading to black behind the high-rises. I'd left my wallet at home, I had nothing but a notebook and a ballpoint in the breast pocket of my shirt and a twenty-rand note in my sock. On the corner of O'Reilly and Fife, where Aubrey Tearle, the hero of my novel in progress, was supposed to have come across an abandoned supermarket trolley and loaded it with his shopping bags full of papers, I made some notes. I was walking Aubrey's route to check the details, doing some retrospective research. I passed the ghosts of the cafés, the Pigalle and the Zürich, the Café Wien and the Café de Paris, and came to the OK Bazaars in Twist Street, where Aubrey had left his trolley in the hands of a security guard before ascending into the quiet interior of the Café Europa. I couldn't remember when last I'd sat down in

Hillbrow for a coffee. I made some more notes, retraced my steps to Prospect Road and drove home.

Dave has the historian's gift of seeing time whole. On his clock, the millennia are no more than minutes, the individual lifespan is a sharp intake of breath. It is a perspective that knocks the self-importance out of people and restores us to our proper place in the scheme. On the other hand, Dave has the storyteller's gift too, which can make the smallest cup of time overflow.

Not so long ago, he says, in a tone which makes a delicious blend of earnestness and irony, we were all hunter-gatherers. Ten thousand years is nothing on the cosmic calendar. This explains why certain kinds of landscape appeal to us so strongly. A meadow sweeping down to a river, a view from the patio over a rolling lawn, a spruit at the bottom of the yard, a koppie on which to loll, with the veld streaming away to the horizon – vistas like these call to our hunter-gatherer hearts.

We are sitting on my stoep. A thunderstorm has just fumed away over the skyline, leaving behind a long smear of cloud. Now the sun dips below this cloud and animates every surface with golden light. The keels of the clouds are ablaze. The falls of rust-red stone on Langermann Kop are as vivid as coals, they seem to glow from within like paper bags holding lit candles, the veld grasses turn to coral.

In Joburg now, Dave goes on, the hunter-gatherer is in the ascendancy. In fact, African cities everywhere are filled with roamers, intent on survival, plucking what they can at the road-side. When people steal the wheels off our cars at night, or scale our walls and make off with the garden furniture, or uproot plants on the embankments beside the freeway, and we raise a hue and cry about law and order and respect for property rights, it's like the Khoikhoi accusing the San of stealing their cattle.

20 Stop Crime
    For peace of mind I secure
    your car while you shop
    For a donation I guard your car
    If harassed by guard, phone number on reverse side
    S.O.B. No: ......
    Guard Name: ......
    This guard is scanned for criminal and security purposes
    We also do functions and house parties

21 During my first conversation with Eddie, when I was new in
    the neighbourhood, I admired his gladioli, which were in
    bloom. He said I should come back in the last week of May and
    he would lift some bulbs for me. He knew my garden well. He
    had been a frequent visitor in my house, way back, when Mrs
    Williams (I think he said) lived there. He remembered when her
    daughter got married, there was a reception in the garden, quite
    unusual in those days. I had good soil for glads.

    Once they reach a certain age, it is difficult to see the child
    in most people. Eddie is one of the exceptions. Although he was
    nearly eighty when we met, the boy in him was still there,
    ghosting through from a black-and-white past. He had moved
    into Blenheim Street long before I was born. His own children,
    he told me, pointing to the house, had been born under this
    roof. These same children, now scattered across the Reef, were
    trying to persuade him to move. They said he shouldn't be living
    on his own, what with the area going to the dogs, and he
    needed taking care of. But he was quite capable of looking after
    himself. Still, he might take them up on the offer, one of these
    days, for *their* sake, if he could get the right price for the place. It
    might be nice for his daughters, too. He could spend a couple of
    months with each of them in turn and do some handiwork to
    earn his keep. He was always working on his house, there was
    always something to patch or paint. He thought nothing of

hanging off the end of a ladder to repaint a gutter.

One year, he decided to put all the leftover pots of paint in his garage to good use by painting a mural on his garden wall. It is the ugliest mural in the whole city: a basket of flowers; a dog with mad eyes and spiky whiskers; a dim-witted sun, with a wry mouth and a set of stiff rays standing out like a bad haircut; a bird of paradise perched on one of the sunbeams; a red-brick wishing-well.

The tenants of the semi-detached at 21/21a Kitchener Avenue have started a shop in one of the rooms of their house. A hand-painted sign rigged on top of a tilting carport says: COCA-COLA, BREAD, MILK. It is unclear where the shop is, exactly, but through an oval window, feint-ruled by venetian blinds, one can make out what seems to be a hairdressing salon. Perhaps it was for the convenience of their customers that the proprietors of these businesses spray-painted the numbers of their house on the wall of the property. The numbers appear to either side of the gate, crooked black digits scrawled across three or four courses of yellow brick, 21 to the left, 21a to the right. A short path leads to the house where the number 21a appears again, ambiguously, spoiling the symmetry, on the central pillar of the stoep.

These numbers incensed Branko. The first time he saw them he started fuming, and he cannot pass the house without commenting. You'd think they'd been put there to offend him.

'But what is it?' I ask him. 'Why does it bother you so much? Why can't you leave it alone?'

'On a brick wall!' he says. 'How could they?'

(They. Branko, being a bit of a racist, means: blacks. The blacks.)

'It's just a garden wall, for God's sake,' I say. 'There's nothing special about it.'

'You don't take an aerosol and spray numbers on a *brick* wall. Even a child knows that. That's it: they're like badly behaved

41

children drawing on the bedroom walls with their wax crayons. They've defaced their own property, they've vandalized themselves. What kind of people are they? Go on, you explain it to me.'

23   With just six weeks left on the millennial clock, a Johannesburg computer specialist claimed that he had been savagely bitten in an attempted car hijacking. The 40-year-old man, who did not wish to be named in the newspaper report on the crime, was stopped at a traffic light in the early hours of the morning, with his car window slightly open. Two thieves reached into the vehicle and released the central locking mechanism. Then they both jumped into the car and began biting him. 'The one in front attacked his arm and bit it all the way up while the other started biting his neck and back, both of them drawing blood as they bit him.' The driver managed to get out of the car, but his assailants pursued him and continued to bite him. 'One was saying: "You taste good, white boy. I want to bite you more."' Eventually he managed to get back into his car and drive off. The man, who said that being bitten was worse than being attacked with a weapon, underwent medical tests and was given antibiotics and a tetanus injection. 'The doctor said a human bite is very poisonous.'

The *Star* has a policy of not identifying individuals by race in their reporting. Here it makes no difference. Even if the phrase 'white boy' had been omitted, who would doubt that the computer specialist was white and the cannibals were black?

24   As Martin draws up to his garage one afternoon after work, he sees two men standing at his garden door, where there is an alcove in the wall covered by a canopy of green corrugated plastic, an 'improvement' made by the previous owner. His first

thought is that they're up to no good, but when they do not take flight at the approach of his car, he thinks again. They must be waiting for someone to answer the doorbell. Perhaps they're looking for Cynthia? Then he suddenly understands the body language: they're taking a piss.

The men glance his way. One of them is wearing a denim jacket, the other has a sky-blue cap with something written on it. The one in the cap makes a remark, the other nods. They go on pissing against the door.

An unfamiliar feeling takes hold of Martin. It drains through his body, he says, like cold water. It is rage. His hand drops onto the Gorilla, which he keeps on the floor beside his seat, and closes round it like a club. But he does not get out of the car, because there is another feeling too, which even this caustic anger cannot scour out of him. Fear.

The man in the jacket zips up his pants and lolls against the wall, while the other one finishes. Martin glowers at them and shakes his head. He wants them to feel his disgust. But he's afraid that even this gesture might provoke a confrontation. When the one in the jacket glances at him, with a smirk, he has to look away. They stroll off.

Vicky is smoking a cigarette in the lounge. She jumps as he slams the front door. Before he's even in the room, he's shouting: 'I've had it with this place. These fucking people. They're like animals.'

'What is it?' she says. 'What's happened?'

'Lifting their legs everywhere like dogs. Honestly, I'm sick to death of it. If one more kaffir pushes me, I'll ride over him.' He sees the amazement on his wife's face and tries to check himself, but he cannot. He rages out of the room. She trails after him into the bedroom, trying to calm him, trying to find out what it's all about. 'Look for yourself!' he yells at her. 'Go take a look at your stinking doorstep and then tell me to calm down!'

His incomprehensible mood is turning on her. She goes back to the lounge. He hears her closing the kitchen door.

He changes out of his suit, hurling jacket and tie and shirt into different corners of the room. These soft, yielding things just add to his frustration. Only when a shoe hits the door of the cupboard and leaves a mark does his rage begin to abate. Instead of flowing out of him in a torrent, words freeze on his lips and fall around him – dogs, kaffirs, cunts – and he comes to his senses. He wonders suddenly whether Cynthia is busy with the supper. He flings himself down on the bed like a child, starts up again immediately, and goes to sit at Vicky's dressing table. He would like to cry, as an expression of remorse, but he is filled with nothing but shame. He looks at his white face in the mirror. His lips are in tatters. His mouth tastes of soap.

'You've got every right to be angry,' Vicky says later when they're trying to talk it through. 'It was obviously provocative.'

'Provocative? It was a calculated insult. There's a park three blocks away where you can piss against a fucking bush if you want to. But they choose to piss on my doorstep.'

He's losing his temper again. She says, 'The problem isn't that you're angry, it's the terms you're using to express it. You should have heard yourself.'

In fact, he's astonished at how easily it came to him, the repetitive, fixated language that has always sustained racism. Colonists everywhere have portrayed indigenous people as brutes unable to control their urges. But Martin is not a 'settler'. He's a middle-class professional, a fourth-generation South African, a political liberal, a democrat. He's not a racist – at least, he's no more of a racist than anyone else, as he always says. He gets irritable, for good reason. He hates the mess, the clutter, the disregard for other people and their property. But he can distinguish between the unthinking behaviour of an individual and the supposed disposition of a race. Now this. *Kaffir?* He can hardly believe this archaic language is lodged in him.

25   Highlands is one of those tiny suburbs most people don't even recognize, but I know someone who lived there as a child forty

years ago, in a block of flats on the very edge of the ridge.

On weekends, he once told me, there would be skokiaan parties on the slopes below, where women sold their home-brew among the bluegums, and a blend of dagga smoke and mbaqanga melodies would drift up on the breeze. Inevitably someone would call the police. The vans would arrive in Hunter Street with squealing tyres and the cops would go chasing after people with their batons, while others lay in wait for the fugitives on Stewart's Drive. White policemen and black party-goers, crashing around in the veld, bawling and swearing. The balconies of the flats offered a grandstand view, and whole families would gather to watch, as if they were at the pantomime.

Once one of the neighbours, vaulting over a couch in his haste to catch every minute of the entertainment, cracked his skull on the keystone of an archway and had to be taken away in an ambulance.

Herman Charles Bosman shot dead his stepbrother in the family home in Bellevue on a Saturday night in 1926. The house at 19 Isipingo Street was pointed out to me one day by my friend Louise, as we drove past on the way to my flat in Webb Street (the extension of Isipingo on the Yeoville side of Bezuidenhout Avenue). After that, I hardly ever passed by there without being reminded of murder.

As an admirer of Bosman's work, I thought that people should be made aware of this historic site. I imagined a marker; nothing brassy, mind you, just a simple tablet, like those paving stones that carry the impress of the manufacturer. The spot should be marked on the tourist maps as a place of interest, I thought. Death by shooting was less common in those days, in my suburb at least, and seemed more benign. Bosman himself had given it a romantic sheen. Today I would want a map that is more complete, more representative, recording every violent death on the Witwatersrand, above ground and below, by axe and blade and bullet. What a title deed to despair it would be, this map of the city of the dead, cross-stitched in black, crumpling under the weight of sorrow as you struggle to unfold it on the dining-room table.

Louise finds this morbid. Why not a map of the living? she asks. Why not a map showing every room, in every house, in every street of this bursting city, where a life began?

27   *Homemade (Roll 1)*

a brazier. a 25-litre drum – BEETLE RESIN – with triangular holes punched through it (the tines of a garden fork?). an aureole of ash and cinders on the pavement, when the brazier has been carried away. a black sun of burnt grass on the yellow verge. a cob with blackened kernels caught in its teeth. stainless-steel shelving from gutted fridges, planks from construction sites encrusted with dried cement, splintered chipboard, printed metal sheets from bus shelters – 'It's a pleasure dealing with the professionals' – estate agents' placards, lengths of angle-iron chained to a no-parking sign. an apple box full of the green spearheads of mielie leaves and the golden shag of their plucked beards. a wire fence brown with rust, wavy as fishnet. a grey-paper shopping bag with the stars and stripes on it. rows of plastic plates arranged on paving stones like counters in a board game. the broken propellor of a banana skin. a canvas awning with its aluminium legs moored to rocks. exhaust pipes and baffles dangling like the day's catch on a line strung between two bluegums. a flattened cardboard carton – FIVE ROSES QUALITY TEA. a window pane glazed with twentieth-century news. the driver's seat of a car standing on its metal runners like a sleigh. a silver bucket with a rag wrung hard as a root in its bottom. a white plastic milk crate like an architect's model in a drift of red sand. a green plastic garden chair, with one leg missing, propped on a paint tin – WALL & ALL. a greasy mattress with a trumpet flower fallen upon it like an omen – 'It's starting to

46

look like a township around here.' cardboard fruit trays stacked into spirals like gigantic snail shells. two gigantic snail shells in the fists of a black woman. a black woman. a brazier

My people are islanders. I am happy enough on the edge of the city, combing its long shores while the weather drives currents through the veld. My English blood makes me go clockwise, the rest urges me the other way around.

As we sat in the kitchen of Jeff's house in Rockey Street, drink- ing beer and eating prawn rolls from his uncle's restaurant in Chinatown, he shared with Branko and me the scheme for his next artistic project: a wall of remembrance.

The city is passing away, said Jeff, even as we speak, and everyone in it, including ourselves. We must build ourselves a memorial while there is still time. Every person in the Greater Johannesburg area, identified by the voters' roll, must be required to donate an object to the artist for use in the work. This object, which shall be no larger than a standard brick, will be enclosed in due course in a transparent resin block of those very dimensions. These object-enclosing bricks will be used in turn to construct a wall. The Great Wall of Jeff.

There and then, with a feverish sense of our own impending demise, we began to work out the costs. Or rather, because Branko insisted that we be realistic, the extent of the funds we would have to raise. 'Europe is awash with cash for installations and stuff like that,' said Jeff. 'Asia unfortunately not. An input from the Mainland would be good – but Taiwan is out of the question.'

'Let's say you manage to raise the money for a mountain of resin and a sea of glue,' said Branko. 'The objects will still be a major headache. How on earth will you get people in this greedy town to give things away?'

'But we're not looking for diamond rings and Krugerrands,' said Jeff, 'although I'll bet we get a couple of them. We're looking for any little thing the donor can be induced to part with. It could be nothing more than a button or a piece of string. Everyone has something they could live without.'

In the small hours, when we had broken out the whisky, we did the quantity surveying, totting up the number of bricks in a ten-metre length of wall, two metres high, two courses thick. Jeff fetched the calculator his brother had sent him from Hong Kong for his birthday. Later we moved on to the likely numbers of everyday objects – keys, coins, lapel badges, pencil sharpeners. Even later we worked through the conventional body parts – appendixes, gallstones, wisdom teeth – and the run-of-the-mill fetishes.

I had started out thinking this was one of those artistic projects that would be easier to realize on paper than in the world. It had been on the tip of my tongue to offer to write it down, to work the idea up into a scrap of fiction, relieving Jeff of the responsibility of having to pretend that practical steps were necessary. But I came away convinced that the Great Wall of Jeff belonged in the city. I even had my eye on a patch of parkland in Bertrams for the construction site.

30 The next morning Branko phoned to say that he had come to his senses and wanted nothing more to do with this mad scheme. Frankly, I was relieved. Once my sensible sibling, with his litany of costs and constraints, was out of the picture, we would be free to build as we pleased. And, indeed, the scheme immediately took an interesting new direction.

'Calling it an art work will create the wrong impression,' I said to Jeff. 'People are so ill-disposed towards art. Let's make it a public works project.'

'What difference will that make?'

'We'll employ brick-makers, we'll create jobs, the whole thing will be voluntary and transparent. Instead of dictating to people, we'll ask them nicely to donate the materials, it will improve the quality of the objects. Anyone can be coerced into parting with a safety pin. But what's the point? Let's say the whole initiative is aimed at those people who wish to belong to it, who have an active desire to be commemorated.'

It was this line of thinking that introduced the question of values.

Jeff's idea: 'Why not have them donate an object that really means something to them. And let them put a price on it, an estimate of its worth, which we can etch upon the brick along with their names. This is the Golden City, after all, the capital of buying and selling. And what is a city if not a showcase of subjective attachments?'

My idea: 'Why a wall? Half the city has already vanished behind walls. Even a semi-transparent one can only make things worse. Why not something useful?'

At which point there arose before my mind's eye a building that owed something to the Crystal Palace, and something else to the Transvaal Museum in Paul Kruger Street, Pretoria, and something more to the OK Bazaars in the Eastgate Mall. It was the Hyperama of Sentimental Value. I was walking along its shiny corridors, surrounded on all sides by a peculiarly impenetrable transparency, where objects hung suspended, attached by nothing but space to the names of the people who once loved them.

Occasionally, when Louise was teaching at the Twilight 31 Children's Shelter in Esselen Street and I was working as an editor at Ravan Press in O'Reilly Road, we would meet for lunch at the Florian in Hillbrow. If the weather was good, we sat outside on the first-floor balcony. Then she would slip her arms out of her paint-stained overalls and tie the sleeves in a big bow across her chest, so that she could feel the sun on her bare shoulders. Despite the chocolate-dipped letters of its Venetian name, the Florian offered English boarding-house fare: chops and chips, liver and onions with mashed potatoes, mutton stews and long-grained rice. We drank beer, although it was sure to make us sleepy, watched the traffic in the street below, and stayed away from work longer than the lunch hour we were entitled to.

The discovery of something unexpected about the world always filled her with an infectious wonder. Once, she tugged me over to the balcony railings at the Florian to point out the iron covers on the water mains set into the pavements. Did I know the spaces below these covers, where the meters are housed? Well, the poor people of Joburg, the street people – we did not call them 'the homeless' in those days – the tramps, car parkers and urchins, used them as cupboards! They stored their winter wardrobes there and the rags of bedding they used at night, they preserved their scraps of food, their perishables, in the cool shade, they banked the empty bottles they collected for the deposits. It tickled her – she laughed out loud, just as if the idea had poked her in the ribs – that such utilitarian spaces should have been appropriated and domesticated, transformed into repositories of privacy for those compelled to live their lives in public. Any iron cover you passed in the street might conceal someone's personal effects. There was a maze of mysterious spaces underfoot, known only to those who could see it. And this special knowledge turned them into the privileged ones, made them party to something in which we, who lived in houses with wardrobes and chests of drawers, and ate three square meals a day, could not participate. Blind and numb, we passed over these secret places, did not even sense them beneath the soles of our shoes. How much more might we be missing?

The food came. While we ate, I began to argue with her about the 'cupboards' and what they represented, as if it were my place to set her straight about the world.

'It's pathetic,' I said, 'that people are so poor they have to store their belongings in holes in the ground.'

'No it's not. It's pathetic when people don't care about themselves, when they give up. These people are resourceful, they're making a life out of nothing.'

'It's like a dog burying a bone,' I said.

'Oh, you'll never understand.'

When we'd finished our lunch and were walking down Twist Street, I wanted to lift up one of the covers to check the contents of the cavity beneath, but she wouldn't hear of it. It wasn't right to go prying into people's things.

'What about the meter-readers?' I asked. 'Surely they're always poking their noses in?'

'That's different,' she said. 'They're professionals. Like doctors.'

'They probably swipe the good stuff,' I insisted.

'Nonsense. They have an understanding.'

Then we parted, laughing. She went back to the children and I went back to the books. And this parting, called to mind, has a black edge of mourning, because she was walking in the shadow of death and I am still here to feel the sun on my face.

Ten years later, the domestic duty of a tap washer that needs replacing takes me outside into Argyle Street to switch off the mains. There is a storm raging in from the south, the oaks in Blenheim Street are already bowing before its lash, dropping tears as hard as acorns. I stick a screwdriver under the rim of the iron cover and lever it up. In the space beneath I find: a brown ribbed jersey, army issue; a red flannel shirt; a small checked blanket; two empty bottles – Fanta Grape and Lion Lager; a copy of *Penthouse*; a blue enamel plate; a clear plastic bag containing some scraps of food (bread rolls, tomatoes, oranges). Everything is neatly arranged. On one side, the empties have been laid down head to toe, the plate balanced across them to hold the food; on the other, the blanket has been folded, the shirt and jersey side by side on top of it, the magazine rolled up between. In the middle, behind a lens of misted glass, white numbers on black drums are revolving, measuring out a flood in standard units.

I kneel on the pavement like a man gazing down into a well, with this small, impoverished, inexplicably orderly world before me and the chaotic plenitude of the Highveld sky above.

32   Walking along Viljoen Street in Lorentzville one day, I saw a black man in overalls sitting on the kerb, taking off a pair of broken boots and putting on a brand-new pair of running shoes, which he had just finished lacing. I was reminded of Douglas Spaulding, the American kid in Ray Bradbury's *Dandelion Wine*, who exchanged his winter shoes for a pair of Litefoot sneakers at Mr Sanderson's shoe store. Douglas cleverly persuaded the proprietor to try on a pair of Litefoots himself, to *feel* how quick and lively they rendered the wearer. Not only was the old man moved to give the boy the sneakers at a discount, he offered him a job selling shoes in his emporium. While I was recalling this, the black man finished tying his laces and walked quickly away with a spring in his step, leaving the old boots side by side in the gutter. The whole episode seemed like a parable about the dignity of labour, the moving congruence of hard work rewarded by simple but intense pleasures. I went on my way with a lump in my throat.

A few blocks further there was a commotion on the pavement outside Seedat's Outfitters in Kitchener Avenue. A passer-by had flung a brick through the plate-glass window and snatched some goods from the display. The brick was still lying there among the dusty satin drapes, chrome-plated pedestals and handwritten price-tags. It was a wonderful brick, a model brick, with three round holes through it the size of one-rand coins, filled with chips of broken glass.

33   Out of the blue, the tenants of 32 Albemarle Street were evicted. Their furniture piled on the pavement made it look like a

forced removal. In passing, for the record, I counted ten double beds, and not much else.

Branko's explanation of why people looking for the Marymount 34 always got lost on my corner revealed something crucial about movement through the city. The way and the walker (and the driver, too, if he has time for such things) are in conversation. The 'long poem of walking' is a dialogue. Ask a question of any intersection – say you are looking for company, the centre of things, water, the road less travelled – and it will answer, not always straightforwardly, allowing a quirk of the topography, the lie of the land, a glimpse of a prospect to nudge you one way or the other. This conversation is one of the things that makes city walking interesting, and one of the masters of the art was Dickens.

Long before he invented London, Dickens knew that cities exist primarily so that we can walk around in them. The *Sketches by Boz*, his earliest published writings, collected for the first time in 1836, no less than the essays published thirty years later as *The Uncommercial Traveller*, arose largely from such wanderings. In each of the books there is a piece devoted to walking in the city at night. 'The Streets – Night' starts with the declaration that the streets of London, 'to be beheld in the very height of their glory, should be seen on a dark, dull, murky winter's night', and the descriptions that follow are confined mainly to the savoury side of midnight, to muffin men and kidney-pie merchants and playgoers. In the later piece, 'Night Walks', the insomniac author, in the figure of 'Houselessness', walks and walks and walks, from midnight to daybreak, and presents a fuller and more sombre picture of the city.

Yet even as he tells us how quiet and empty the streets are when the last drunkards turned out by the publicans have staggered away, and the late pie men and hot-potato men have gone off trailing sparks, and even as he yearns for a sign of company, there seems to be life and light around every corner: the toll-keeper at his fire on Waterloo Bridge, the 'fire and light' of the Newgate turnkeys, a watchman with a lantern. In his most threatening encounters with other creatures – a furtive figure withdrawing into a shadowed doorway, a ragged beggar – they are as suspicious and frightened as he. In a coffee room at Covent Garden, where there is toast and coffee to be had at an early hour, he comes across the most alarming figure of all, a man who produces a meat pudding from his hat, stabs it with his knife, tears it apart with his fingers and gobbles it down. It is enough to make one envious, that the darkest villains of the piece should be possessed of such extravagant habits and showy appetites.

When daylight comes and the streets begin to fill with work-men and hawkers, Dickens admits what we have begun to sus-pect – that he and the streets have not just been conversing, but arguing, that it has taken him some effort, and given him some pleasure, to pursue his solitary way: 'And it is not, as I used to think, going home at such times, the least wonderful thing in London, that in the real desert region of the night, the houseless wanderer is alone there.'

Dickens was blessed to live in a city that offered the walker 'miles upon miles of streets' in which to be lonely and 'warm company' at every turn once his loneliness had been satisfied. Moreover, to live in a city that collaborated enthusiastically in its own invention. I live in a city that resists the imagination. Or have I misunderstood? Is the problem that I live in a fiction that unravels even as I grasp it?

A stranger, arriving one evening in the part of Joburg I call home, would think that it had been struck by some calamity, that every last person had fled. There is no sign of life. Behind the walls, the houses are ticking like bombs. The curtains are drawn tight, the security lights are glaring, the gates are bolted. Even the cars have taken cover. Our stranger, passing fearfully through the streets, whether in search of someone with open hands of whom he might ask directions or merely of someone to avoid in the pursuit of solitude, finds no one at all.

The range of steering locks available in South Africa is impressive – the Wild Dog, the MoToQuip anti-theft lock, the Twistlok, the SL2 AutoLok, the Eagle Claw by Yale, the Challenger... All these locks work on the same principle: they are attached to the steering wheel and immobilize the vehicle by preventing the wheel from being turned.

The locks also have the same basic design. There is a hardened steel shaft and an extendable bar. The two parts are connected by a locking ratchet mechanism and each part is furnished with a U-shaped hook or 'claw'. To engage the lock, you place the shaft diametrically across the steering wheel, with the bar retracted and the shaft claw around the rim. Then you extend the bar until the second claw fits around the opposite side of the rim. The ratchet engages automatically and locks the bar in place. If an attempt is made to turn the steering wheel now, the protruding end of the bar strikes the passenger seat, windscreen or door. To disengage the device, you insert the key in the lock and retract the bar, freeing the claws on both sides.

In some devices, the U-shaped hook on the shaft is replaced by a corkscrew hook, which is twisted around the rim of the steering wheel before the bar is engaged. The Twistlok, for instance, has such a hook, which is called the 'pigtail end'.

The selling points of the various locks are similar. They are made of tough, hardened steel which cannot be drilled, sawn or bent, and they are coated with vinyl to protect the interior fittings. They are easy to install, thanks to the automatic locking system, and highly visible to thieves; to heighten their visibility, and therefore their deterrent value, they are often brightly coloured. They have pick-resistant locks and high-security keys: the MoToQuip has 'cross point' keys; the Challenger has a 'superior circular key system'; and Yale offers a 'pin tumbler locking system' with ten thousand different key combinations and exerts strict control over the issuing of duplicates, by approved service centres only.

Some of these products draw explicitly on the symbolism of the predatory animal. The Eagle Claw, for instance, suggests a bird of prey, a raptor with the steering wheel in its clutches. The logo of the Wild Dog depicts a snarling Alsatian, more rabid and vicious than the conventional guard dog. The association with wild animals known for their speed, strength or ferocity is also found in other areas of the security industry: tigers, eagles and owls appear on the shields of armed response companies, and rhinoceroses and elephants in the logos of companies that supply electrified fencing and razor wire.

36   The day after I acquired my new car, a bottle-green Mazda Midge, my dad arrived on my doorstep. He was carrying a long package wrapped in mistletoe paper, although Christmas was a long way off. I knew at once what was in this package, but I pretended that I did not.

My dad works in the motor trade and I have always respected his opinions about cars. He gave the Mazda a thorough check-up, doing all the things men do to determine the quality of a second-hand vehicle – kicking the tyres, bouncing up and down on the fenders to test the shock absorbers, looking in the cubbyhole, jiggling the steering wheel, gazing under the hood. He announced that I had made a sensible purchase. Then he gave me the present. It was a Gorilla.

He showed me how it worked, engaging and disengaging the device with practised ease. When it was my turn, the lock suddenly seemed like a test of perceptual intelligence, an educational toy of some kind. My fingers felt thick and clumsy, my hand-eye coordination had deserted me. The 'pigtail' kept slipping off the rim, like one of those magician's hoops that has a secret join in it.

Finally I managed to engage the Gorilla.

'Don't worry, you'll get used to it,' he said. 'In the meantime, I have a couple of tips for you. Before you do anything else, you want to engage the standard steering lock that comes with the car. Just turn the wheel anticlockwise until it clicks in.

'Never install the device so that it's touching one of the windows. I know a guy who did that, and the bar expanded in the sun and cracked his windscreen.

'Then you must find a place to store the lock when it's not in use. I suggest you put it down here next to the seat. It's out of the way and there's no danger of it getting caught under the pedals.

'Finally, you need to put a drop of oil in here from time to time. Just a drop, very occasionally. You don't want to get it on the upholstery.

'Right. Let's see you do it again.'

The Gorilla is the best of the breed. It is made in one solid piece. There is no ratchet and no extension; instead the lock, like a jointed metal jaw, slides up and down on a single bar. This bar is made of naked stainless steel, harsh on the eye and cold to the touch – until it is exposed to the sun, whereupon it gets hot enough to blister the skin. The 'pigtail' is bright red. The shiny metal bar is not coated with protective plastic and so the device is leaner than the average lock, but if anything it looks stronger. It has nothing to hide. One is never tempted to wonder what material is concealed beneath the plastic. This is 'super hard steel', as the packaging declares, designed to put an end to the 'monkey business of car theft'.

The brutal style of the device is echoed in one of the manufacturer's slogans: 'There's no substitute for brute force.' The pun on 'brute force' furthers a play of meanings already suggested by the trade name 'Gorilla'. Brute force is unthinking material force: there is no substitute for unbending steel. But it is also unfeeling animal force: there is no substitute for a powerful, dull-witted beast like a 'Gorilla'.

In English, mechanical devices are very commonly given the names of animals. In mechanics and mining, for instance, there are countless devices designated as 'dogs'. A 'dog' may be any

37

form of spike, rod or bar with a ring, hook or claw for gripping, clutching or holding something. 'Dogs' form part of machines used in mines, sawmills and engineering works. 'Firedogs' are used to support wood in a fireplace, 'raft dogs' to hold together the logs forming a raft. Various machines and implements are also named 'monkeys', either arbitrarily or because of a supposed resemblance between the object and the animal. A 'monkey' is a crucible used in the manufacture of glass, for instance, or a weight used in the manufacture of iron. In the nautical environment, 'monkey' usually indicates that something has a peculiar use or location; it may also indicate that something is easy or simple. A 'monkey link', for instance, is an easily inserted repair link for a chain. This may be part of the derivation of 'monkey wrench', a tool which is a close cousin of the Gorilla.

The ambiguous identity of a single device as dull object and dumb animal is captured in the logo of the Gorilla, which shows a stylized steering wheel gripped by two huge, humanoid paws, with the shaggy suggestion of an animal body in the background. Attaching this particular lock to the steering wheel is like leaving a Gorilla sitting in the driver's seat. Elsewhere on the packaging we read: 'Find your car where you left it – get a "Gorilla" to protect it.' This slogan hints at a more covert layer of meaning. Colloquially a 'gorilla' is a powerfully built, brutish, aggressive man. So the device may be seen as a sort of simian watchman.

38   One former owner of our house was a DIY man and fond of wood. The house is full of his handiwork. He must have been very tall, Minky says. Her feet don't touch the floor when she sits on the window seat, and the rails of the built-in cupboards are so high she can hardly reach. Even his little touches were large ones – the door handles were made for a heavyweight's fist, the window sills would hold a set of encyclopedias.

On the inside of the wall beside the front gate he installed a letter-box for a person with large appetites, someone capable of sustaining extensive correspondences and making extravagant purchases by mail order. On the outside was a brass slot, with a peak like a postman's cap for keeping out the rain, covering an aperture in the wall. That slot was generous enough to admit a rolled newspaper or a thickly stuffed A4 envelope.

A small letterbox is more than an inconvenience, it is the mark of a mean nature. But if our letterbox had been smaller, if there had been less brass in it, it may have been less attractive to a thief. One night some scavenger after scrap stuck a crowbar under an edge of the slot and broke it out of the plaster. Now the box is filling up with dust and dead leaves. The hardware man at Tile City offered us a replacement in plastic, not as durable as brass but unlikely to be stolen. People were coming in all day, he said, wanting plastic numbers for their gates.

Afterwards Minky and I took a walk through the neighbourhood, from one shadowy number of unvarnished wood to another of unpainted plaster, following the trail the thieves blazed up and down the blocks, breaking brass numbers off doors and walls.

In the front door of our house is a hinged flap marked LETTERS, left over from a time when the postman, unhindered by locks and barbs and security grilles, could open the garden gate, come up the path, climb the steps, cross the stoep, and drop the letters through a slot onto the hallway floor.

Gold was discovered on the Witwatersrand in the winter of 1886. Until then the veld had offered no more than grazing for a handful of cattle farmers, but soon it was dotted with wagons, tents and reed huts, as gold-seekers poured into the area. Within three or four years a town of brick houses, offices, hotels and government buildings sprang up, and within a generation the city was home to half a million people.

Commissioner Street, the backbone of Johannesburg, follows

the old wagon track between two of the first mining camps, from Jeppestown in the east to Ferreirasdorp in the west. So the city's spine was fused to the gold-bearing reef that called it into life. Today, going down Commissioner into the high-rise heart of the city, I am reminded that here we are all still prospectors, with a digger's claim on the earth beneath our feet. Where Commissioner passes the Fairview Fire Station, cracks have appeared in the tar, long, ragged creases following the curve of the road. Here and there chunks of tar have broken loose and rusted steel glimmers in the roadbed. The tramlines, tarred over in the early sixties, coming back to the surface.

40   On the pavement outside No. 10 Blenheim: a tall man whose splattered overall and abstracted demeanour spoke of long experience in house-painting. He had spread a strip of plastic at the foot of the garden wall, beneath our Ndebele mural, and was stirring a tin of paint with a stick. The mural must have been two or three years old by then. He's touching up the cracks, I told myself hopefully, although it was obvious what he was really doing. As I drew near, he laid the stick across the top of the tin and went to stand on the other side of the street. Like a woodsman sizing up a tree, just before he chopped it down.

I couldn't watch. I went on to the Gem to fetch the paper. Coming home, I nearly made a detour along Albemarle Street to avoid the scene entirely, but it had to be faced.

He had started on the left. He was hacking into the pattern, obliterating it with extravagant swipes of the roller. Standing back, from time to time, to admire his handiwork. As if there was anything to be seen but an act of vandalism. The man must be a brute, I thought. It would be a man, too, the very antithesis of the woman who had painted the mural. I tried to remember her, but she had faded in my memory. I saw a middle-aged woman with a blanket knotted about her, wearing neck rings and a beaded headdress – but this was Esther Mahlangu, the painter of the BMW, whose photograph had been in the news-papers many times! In any event, they were not opposites. She was not an artist and he was not a vandal. They were simply people employed by the owners of a suburban house to perform a task. What the one had been employed to do, the other had now been employed to undo.

It was unthinkable that the same person could have com-manded both tasks. The house had been on the market for some time and my theory was that it had finally changed hands. The new owner was remaking the place in his own style. Ndebele murals are an acquired taste, after all.

My brother Branko had a less charitable interpretation. They haven't found a buyer, he said, and it's no bloody wonder. They're finally taking the estate agent's advice: paint it white. It's a dictum. Matches every lounge suite.

However, they did not paint it white. They painted it a lemony yellow with green trim, a petrol-station colour scheme. It took a couple of coats; after the first one, you could still see the African geometry developing, like a Polaroid image, as the paint dried.

Having missed the opportunity to document the birth of the mural through a lack of foresight, I now lacked the inclination to document its demise. This would make a wonderful film, I said to myself. But I did not call my friends the film-makers. I did not rush home to fetch a camera. I did not even take out a pad and pencil like a cub reporter. I just stood on the other side of the street and watched for a while, as the design vanished stroke by stroke, and then I went home with a heavy heart.

Here he is, the security guard at Gem Pawn Brokers, relaxing 41
outside. It is the end of the working day and I'm heading to the Jumbo Liquor Market for some beer. He has already helped his colleagues to carry in the jumble of pine tables and metal shelves displayed on the pavement today as 'specials', but a single

chair has been left behind in which he can lounge until the doors are shut. When Mannie comes out with the key, the guard will carry in this last item, a fat, balding Gomma Gomma arm-chair, and oversee the locking and barring.

He always ignores me, though I can tell that he recognizes me, passing by, just as I recognize him, sitting there. It irks me, this denial of the everyday pleasantries that set people at ease. Why won't he acknowledge me? Is it the neighbourhood that makes people so guarded? I have been shopping in the Gem Supermarket for years and still no one greets me at the till. Any hint of friendliness is met with brooding suspicion, as if it must be a prelude to asking for credit. The scrawny manager with his support hose and his Fair Isle jerseys, the slant-eyed women and their toffee-stained children, they all look through you if you're on the wrong side of the counter, sloping their shoulders defen-sively. After ten years of patronizing the Jumbo, I once found myself short of a couple of rand on a bottle of wine. I offered to make up the balance the next day, but the cashier wouldn't have any of it. The manager was summoned. Grudgingly, he produced a two-rand coin from his wallet and put it in my hand, informed me that I was now indebted to him personally rather than the business, as if that would guarantee my honesty, and went away with a long face. The shopkeepers have reason to insult us, I sup-pose, for people are quick to take advantage. But what could I possibly want from the security guard at Gem Pawn Brokers?

An experiment. I greet him one afternoon, putting my heart into it. He returns the favour. *Hello! Hello.* It is no more than an echo, but it gives me some pleasure. *Hello! Hello.*

After a month of this game, a follow-up experiment be-comes necessary and is made one afternoon. I don't say any-thing; he keeps silent too. The next day I try to catch his eye as usual, but he looks away, bewildered and resentful. He thinks I'm up to something. I had no idea my experiment would produce this irrevocable reversal. Now, when he sees me coming, he draws back into himself and glazes over. Even if I throw out a cheery greeting, he pretends he hasn't heard.

The grand old cinemas of Johannesburg, the bioscopes, were driven out of business years ago by the multiplexes. Most of the defunct bioscopes have been appropriated by people who own junk shops. Perhaps they were the first to arrive at the Plaza or the Regal or the Gem when the curtain fell, hungry for spills of red velvet and rows of seats joined at the hip, and so much echoing space proved irresistible. You can trundle a piano through the wide doorways and pile things to the rafters, or even put in a mezzanine to double the floor space, as they've done at the Plaza. If there are windows at all, they are small and high, and do not even need bars.

The junk shops, like other businesses in the neighbourhood, take the names of the old establishments, as if it is important to preserve the association. The Plaza Pawn Warehouse in Primrose specializes in outmoded office furniture, a film-noir decor of grey steel desks and filing cabinets, wooden in- and out-trays, adding machines, fans, typists' chairs with chrome-plated frames and imitation-leather cushions. Regal Furnishers opposite the Troyeville Hotel sells plywood bedroom suites and kitchen cabinets. Gem Pawn Brokers buys and sells anything of value, as their sign declares. In its heyday, when the Gem was the grandest bioscope in the eastern suburbs, a back door gave on to a small landing, where the usher could loaf between features smoking a Lucky Strike, gazing over the tiled roof of the Second Church of Christ, Scientist, to the lights of Bez Valley and Bertrams, one ear tuned to the mutter of the spooling picture. Now this doorway is a frozen frame bricked in to keep out thieves.

The alliance of dark cinemas and second-hand goods is a happy one. In this deconsecrated space, objects that would appear lifeless in an ordinary shop throw flickering shadows. The profusion of goods evokes a storehouse rather than a market. These are the cast-off properties of people's lives, mementos of their hopes and failures, and the signs of use that should be offputting seem poignant. A piano stool with a threadbare cushion, a dented toolbox, a Morris chair with cigarette-burned arms, a vellum lampshade dotted with postage stamps, a soda siphon, a bottle-green ashtray in the shape of a fish – there is nothing so tawdry that it is powerless to summon a cast of characters.

The proprietors of junk shops do not care for books, preferring to deal in larger items with a more obvious use and a more determinate value. But inevitably they are saddled with a few volumes. For convenience, a seller might refuse to part with a set of shelves if the dealer won't take their contents, or an odd volume will turn up in a bedside drawer or the bottom of a wardrobe. Usually, there will be a row or two of books somewhere in the shop, on a bookshelf no one wants. If you wish to flip through them, you might have to hang over the back of a couch or kneel in a cramped space. There is no order to these books, their collection was informed by no particular taste. Yet, because of the circumstances in which it is acquired, a bioscope book has a special quality: it is attended by a more vivid retinue of ghosts.

43   *Handwritten (Roll 2)*

The sign is painted on the end of an overhanging roof, in glossy blue enamel on a white ground: Dokotela + Ngaka. Between the two words, a wobbly red cross with a broken arm. And then a telephone number, with its last digit teetering on the edge, its face pressed up against the downpipe from the gutter, while the three digits behind jostle together in an impatient queue.

'It's starting to look like a township around here.'

The township is written in longhand across the printed page of the white city, in felt tip, in chalk, in gaudy heeltaps of enamel. The new services: Dokotela, Pan-African Financial Systems, Siyathuthuka Tavern Ngubane. White eyes appraise these declarations on flaking facades, accompanied by crude drawings of stethoscopes and knives and forks, and put the premises and proprietors in inverted commas: 'Herbalist', 'Moneylender', 'Eating house'…

The white city is made of steel and glass, illuminated from within. It is printed on aluminium hoardings and Perspex sheeting. It is bolted down, recessed and double-glazed, framed and sealed, it is double-sided and laminated, it is revolving in the wind on a well-greased axle.

The township is made of cardboard and hardboard, buckling in the sunlight. It is handpainted on unprimed plaster, scribbled on the undersides of things, on the blank reverses, unjustified, in alphabets with an African sense of personal space, smudged. Tied to a fence with string. leaning against a yield sign. propped up by a brick. secured with a twist of wire. nailed to a tree trunk.

Paiter. Call Tymon. Tell 725 6918.

I turn my gaze from this message, scarcely decipherable in the dusk, to the crisply edged signage of the petrol station across the intersection. The light changes to green. The driver behind, who has never heard the joke about the definition of a split second, leans on his hooter.

On the Blenheim Street facade of the Second Church of Christ,   44
Scientist, between two sets of doors that have never looked quite so inviting since their brass handles were nicked, is a foundation stone inscribed with this plainspoken injunction: • LOVE • On either side of the word, the mason scooped a stud out of the stone. This incidental punctuation keeps an abstract concept, which might otherwise have floated away, pinned to a hard surface. In the bottom right-hand corner, a second, lopsided inscription – 1927 – tips the stone into the course of time.

In a corner of the parking area at the Darras Shopping Centre,   45
near the Engen garage, a man is standing, a tall black man in a suit, a collar and tie, shiny shoes, a hat. He is standing to attention, rigidly upright, with his hands at his sides. A priest or a

teacher, someone who would make a good character witness in a trial. At his feet is a square metre of cardboard and in the centre of it a bathroom scale wrapped in clear plastic. It is pale yellow with a white oval dial. A small white card beside the scale says: 50c.

My God, I think, he could get more than fifty cents for the thing! I should tell him so. I'd give him twenty rand for it myself, if I needed it.

Then the deception occurs to me: there must be a scam involved. When you offer him fifty cents for the scale, he'll say he has another two thousand of them in a warehouse in Heriotdale. Give him a small deposit, say a hundred bucks, and he'll fetch them for you. And that's the last you'll see of your cash. Transparent.

And then, ten paces further, I realize how perfectly simple it is.

46   Strolling home with the morning paper under his arm, Branko passes a salesman dragging a large briefcase. He looks like a salesman anyway, in blazer and flannels, white shirt and striped tie, a door-to-door man lugging a set of samples. Branko feels sorry for him in this heat, trying to give the heavy case an extra little shove with his calf at each step, his free arm sticking out like a wing, pigeon-toed with effort.

At his own door, Branko nearly falls into a hole in the pavement. The iron cover that's supposed to conceal the connection to the water mains is gone. It was here ten minutes ago, when he stepped out to buy the paper. He stands there puzzling.

Shit!

He jams his paper in the letterbox and runs down the street, looking for the man with the case, unsure what he will do with this white-collar criminal when he catches him, but he has already vanished.

Returning from a reception in Sandton, we find ourselves
locked out of the bedroom. I have got into the habit of half-
turning the latch on the inside so that the door doesn't swing
open in the breeze, and now it's clicked shut on its own. At two
in the morning. We phone the Lock King and negotiate a price.
Then we pour ourselves a couple of stiff whiskies and sit in the
lounge to wait. Half an hour later a tough-looking kid and his
blonde girlfriend arrive. She is wearing fluffy pink slippers with
her jeans. While he sets about picking the lock, she leans against
him, rubbing the back of his neck, stroking his forearm. We sit in
our armchairs, in black tie and ball gown, and watch them at
work. They look like thieves.

I'm coming home along Roberts Avenue, when I see Eddie
dithering on the pavement by the substation near the Black
Steer steak house. He's looking up and down Blenheim Street,
walking a step or two downhill and then hurrying back up
again. Homing.

It must be six months since he sold his house and moved,
and this is the first time I've caught sight of him in the old
neighbourhood. I'm pleased to see him, and yet I don't feel like
talking to him. Even in the moment, this impulse strikes me as
uncharitable, but I cannot suppress it. So I stop in the shade of
the fig tree on the corner to watch. He hasn't seen me and he
doesn't seem likely to either; he's too engrossed in his own
dilemma. Up and down, up and down. His pacing is like paging;
he has lost his place in the world. Finally, he goes downhill de-
cisively towards his house. I've seen him do this countless times,
hobbling back from the Gem with a loaf of bread under his
arm, going up the garden path. But he doesn't live here any
more. When he's one door away from his old home, he veers
across to the other pavement and stops, watching from a distance, on the bias. He cannot face it. He starts coming back up
the hill again.

Now a meeting is unavoidable, and I'm suddenly delighted to see him. He's just as pleased to see me: he seizes upon me like a bookmark. But he also looks guilty, as if he's been caught out doing something discreditable. Before I can ask, he starts telling me how much he enjoys it in Germiston. Been gone eight months already, can you believe it? His daughter had business in town today, so she dropped him off. He's been visiting with George at the Black Steer and old Mrs Ferreira. Looking around. George is closing down, did you know that? Mrs Ferreira used to own half the block. Now she's reduced to her place and the place next door, and not even a decent tenant for that.

I let him tell me yesterday's news. Then I ask: 'What's it like to be back? Have we changed?'

We both turn and face down the hill.

'My garden's not looking so good,' he says.

'No.'

'New chap's not much of a gardener.'

'It's a pity.'

'This has always been a beautiful part of town,' he says. 'The streets are so wide, and the oaks are grand, and the houses are set back just right, don't you think? You notice it when you've been away for a while. I was saying to my daughter this morning: There isn't a finer street in Joburg than Roberts Avenue.'

Eddie's mural comes and goes with the seasons; in the summer, it is obscured by the shrubs growing wild in the front garden, in the autumn, when the leaves fall, it reappears to haunt us.

49   Louis Fehler stayed with me in my flat in Webb Street before he emigrated. At the last minute he asked me to keep some papers for him just until he was settled on the other side, and then I was stuck with them. I lugged his blue trommel to half a dozen addresses, cursing him every time. I put it on the bathroom scale

once and it weighed thirty kilos.

When he died I should have surrendered the trunk straight away, but I was curious about its contents. One weekend – I often get round to chores on a Sunday afternoon, like a schoolboy doing his homework – I sawed through the padlock. The first thing I came to was a file called 'Heydays', which turned out to be fragments of an unfinished autobiography. Beneath it lay a dozen cardboard folders containing notes, chronologies, clippings, photographs and letters (including copies of his own).

It was flattering to think of this as a posthumous commission, but I had no interest in being Louis's biographer. He had his admirers and I might have passed the papers on to one of them, but there again the thought of handing over my windfall irked me. So I closed the trommel and put it away. From time to time I'm reminded that this legacy is in my hands, as I was again last week when I started packing up the spare room, and the blue trommel came to light behind the exercise bike and the broken chairs.

It took three days to frame Ilona Anderson's exhibition. Having no workbench or tub, I had to wash the flimsy sheets of glass in the shower, resting the bottom edge on a sponge, then carry them wet to the table in the hallway, where I dried them with crumpled sheets of newspaper. The drawings showed puppets and dolls, made to squirm by many huge, puppet-masterly hands, every surface trembling with theatrical colour, applied as thickly as lipstick or toothpaste, and always on the point of smudging. Three dozen works were finished without a hitch. But on the morning of the opening, a wine glass broke in my hand under the kitchen tap and sliced my forefinger to the bone. It is twenty years since the wound healed, but if a rim of glass even brushes against the scar those livid colours bleed out of my memory.

50

51   Minky's brother Alan phones: 'You won't believe what's happened.' He sounds so dejected that for a moment she thinks someone must have died. He goes on: 'Have you driven down Scott Street lately?' Then she knows, before he tells her: the Scott Street house, where they once lived, has been demolished.

    In his fifty years in Joburg, Alan has lived in four houses, all within walking distance of one another. In fact, when he started jogging, he laid out his route to take him past three of them – Murray Street, Scott Street, William Road. Passing by these landmarks, he would retrace his passage from child, to teenager, to young married man, and return to the present, in Victoria Street, his fourth – and, he says, final – address, more fully himself. But one after the other, over the years, the houses have been knocked down. Scott Street was the last.

    'It's unbelievable,' he says. 'It was there last week and now there's nothing left but the foundations. I'm starting to feel paranoid. It's as if someone is trying to erase me from the record. I half expect to come home from work one day and find my house knocked down.'

    Minky's father built the house in Scott Street in the midsixties, when she and Al were teenagers. He oversaw every step of the construction and spared no cost. Tiles of Italian marble, doorframes of Rhodesian teak. Even the roof-trusses were imported from Canada, because Canadian pine is stronger and straighter.

    'You can't take it with you when you go,' he used to say, 'but you can leave something behind. This house will stand for a hundred years.'

52   The last day of 1998. I stop at the Jumbo Liquor Market in Op de Bergen Street on the way home to buy something for the New Year celebrations. Perhaps I should pick up a bottle of whisky? Or champagne?

    The usual hawkers are gathered on the verandah outside.

The tall cobbler and his pals. For years, he wore a springbok-skin cap, a hand-sewn thing that Crusoe would have given a sack of nails for, with flaps standing up like ears and a peak like a snout. With his bony cheeks and goatee, he looked like a buck himself or a part-time Pan. But then he abandoned the cap in favour of the conventional black imitation leather Tyrolean.

While I'm engaging the Gorilla, a man appears at the window. I've never seen him before. He puts his face close to the two-inch gap between the top of the glass and the frame. A face made in the make-up department: a droll and drunken coloured face below a greasy cloth cap, missing teeth, smashed nose, boozy breath. 'I must watch this car, this place is full of skollies,' he tells me, gesturing vaguely towards the cobbler's circle and then pointing very definitely down Eleanor Street. 'Just last week they stole that car.' The car in question is a bakkie, drawing up that instant outside No. 12, having come the wrong direction up the one-way from Nourse Street. Two men get out of the bakkie and go into the house. What does he mean they stole that car last week? Who would have taken such a battered old pickup? And how did they get it back again so soon? Then logic turns his sentence inside out. He means it's a stolen vehicle. Those are the thieves! Probably a thief himself. Takes one to know one. I barge him aside with the door and go into the bottle store.

Champagne bubbles up again briefly. But I think of the obligatory cork-popping in a year's time, and two years' time, and buy beer instead and a half-jack of J&B.

When I get back to my car, the coloured guy is hanging around on the other side of the street, shamefaced and jumpy, trying hopelessly to disguise his expectation. I dump the packet in the boot. I'm starting to regret my bad temper, starting to feel guilty. It's the season for giving, after all. I call him over and give him five bucks.

Now he wants to earn it, he wants to deserve my generosity. And he wants me to see the point too. 'I'm watching,' he says vehemently, 'I'm watching.' He points to his eyes, forefinger and little finger extended, the other two tucked into his fist by his thumb.

I get into the car.

'I'm watching.'

'Thank you,' I say through the diminishing gap, as I shut the door, 'thank you very much.'

His face is close to the glass again. Talking. Gesturing. Prongs of forefinger and little finger waggling, roving, suggesting tireless vigilance. I stick the key in the Gorilla but it won't disengage: in my haste to get away, I've jammed the lock somehow. He goes on talking. I cannot ignore him. Elias Canetti once said: 'I will be dead when I no longer hear what a person is telling me about himself.' This cannot be what he had in mind. I open the window two inches. His face comes closer. He's tilting it to one side, so that I can see more of it through the gap. He wants me to know who he is, to look at him. He wants me to recognize him when I see him again. His nose is almost inside the car. As if he wants to squeeze in, to seize the hard edges of this opening, pull them wide, and climb through into the sweetly scented interior. When they serviced the car last week, they spilled some green pellets in the ashtray that make it smell like new. New-car scent. I jiggle the Gorilla irritably and it finally pops loose. I put it in its place next to the seat. He's still talking, quickly, urgently, about thieves and cars and honesty and how we all have to work together against the scourge of skelms. Waving his arms around, pointing up and down Eleanor Street. Making peculiarly graceful movements with his hands, palms pressed together, as if he is praying or preparing to dive into a small pool.

I start the car but he won't let me go. He's talking and talking through the gap. Phrases out of the newspapers. Crime wave. rainbow nation. Decent South Africans. standing together. People of God. thieves. liars. love. I start edging away from the kerb, cranking the steering wheel with my left hand and winding up the window with my right. My face is turned to him. We are staring at one another through the narrowing space.

72

'I'm not a security,' he says as the gap closes. 'I'm not a security, I swear, but I wanna work with the people of the land.'

Apie is a wooden steering lock carved by Renier le Roux.   53
Other works in wood by the same sculptor include a spanner
(*Sleutel No. 13*), a security gate (*Welkom Tuis*) and a brick, which
may be used as a doorstop, a weapon or a purse.

In 1998, 107 675 cars were stolen in South Africa (295 cars per   54
day). There were 14 965 cars hijacked (41 per day). The inci-
dence of hijacking was directly related to the efficacy of vehicle
security systems. The increasing application of alarms, electronic
immobilizers, and steering and gear locks, especially to luxury
motor cars, has made it almost impossible to steal an unoccu-
pied, stationary car.

In 1998, a survey by the Labour Research Service in Cape
Town found that the executive directors of South African companies earned an average of R99 916 per month, or R1.2 million
a year, excluding bonuses and other benefits. Executive salaries
were sixty times higher than shop-floor wages. A factory worker
earning R1 800 a month – the average minimum wage – would
have taken five years to earn what the average company director
earned in a month. Yet these workers had to consider themselves
fortunate, because 40 per cent of black South Africans were un-
employed.

In 1999, crime cost South Africa an estimated R30 billion
(R80 million a day). However, crime also created jobs. In the
past two decades, the private security industry has grown faster
than any other economic sector. At the end of August, according
to Martin Schönteich of the Institute for Security Studies, the
official South African Police Service employed 127 000 people.
By contrast, the private security industry employed between

300 000 and 350 000 people, and had an estimated annual turnover of R11 billion.

In August 1999, the prices of new cars available in South Africa ranged from R38 086 for a Fiat Uno Mia to R2 389 000 for a Ferrari 550 Maranello. The prices of steering locks ranged from R59 for the SL2Auto-Lok to R325 for the Gorilla. The price of brown bread was fixed by the government at R1.90 a loaf.

55   My name is ......
      I am a trained Guard to fight Vehicle and Street Crime
      ABACUS Crime Watch
      Endorsed by the Mayor of Greater Johannesburg
      Guards do not receive Wages
      Donation appreciated when parking
      Tip on your return, if satisfied with service
      Have a nice day A/h 972 6897 Cell 082 6896 181

56   The avenues in Bez Valley around First Street are narrow one-ways lined with red-brick factories, workshops and warehouses. In places, brick facades or corrugated-iron walls front directly onto the roadway as in an old city. However, the area is no warren: the avenues are long and straight, the buildings seldom taller than two storeys, the sky above blue and vast. In the south of Johannesburg, in the manufacturing areas like Selby and Village Deep, similar streets are to be found, but none with exactly this atmosphere. The buildings are occupied by small manufacturers of goods like garden furniture, burglar-proofing and fireworks, alongside businesses offering marquees for hire, cured and smoked meats, or geyser repairs – an assortment that is only superficially incongruous.

Dorfman's specializes in corrugated cartons and packaging

materials. The cardboard boxes are stacked flat in towers on wooden pallets or leant together in long rows against the walls, thousands of boxes in dozens of standard sizes, classified alpha-numerically. Most are bundled tightly into fifties or hundreds with plastic straps, as if they would spring into three dimensions without this restraint. Selling is by weight and the new boxes are twice the price of the used ones. The new boxes are generally factory rejects. You will find a minor misalignment in the stapled sides, or a more annoying discrepancy in the dimensions of the flaps, which must be trimmed by hand before the box will fold, or, less often, an error in the printing – and these are the real bargains, of course, because a box with a typo on it is just as useful for moving house as one without.

I need two sizes, something small and sturdy for books, and something larger, flimsier if need be for household effects. A worker shows me the range, folding together samples with the flamboyant ease of a magician making something reappear. I settle for the small B6, which has chevrons on its flaps and four Ls arranged in a square on its sides, like corners in an album where a photograph has fallen out, all printed in red; and the larger D14, which is absolutely plain. We lug the boxes to the scale next to the office. Seventeen kilos. The scale is calibrated to five hundred.

'Anything else, sir?' They have self-adhesive tape in thirty- or fifty-metre rolls, clear or brown, masking tape, double-sided tape; bubble wrap by the metre; sisal, nylon, twine; plastic and steel strapping. They have labels, staples and pots of glue, but no mothballs.

There is an animal smell in the air, a gluey effusion of hoof and horn. It suits this uneasy place. The boxes are in an unnat-ural state, mere suggestions of their fully assembled selves. So many cubic metres of space collapsed into square ones, so many roomfuls of compressed air in every corner. Space in captivity seems as full of explosive potential as a fireworks factory.

57 The windows of the house at No. 58 Kitchener Avenue have been blinded by black film. There could be a funeral parlour behind that morbid porch. An all-seeing eye, the Masonic sign of the defunct neighbourhood watch, peers out through the burglar-proofing. The garden wall is chocolate brown. On either side of the gate there are decorative patterns in the brickwork, holes in the shape of a diamond, five holes across at its widest point, ranging down to a single hole above and below. I am compelled to make the calculation: twenty-five holes in total.

As I pass this house one afternoon, on my island walk, a small object comes into focus. In the very centre of one of these diamonds is a tiny model of a man. A plastic figure from toy-town, as tall as my thumb, standing in the aperture as if in a doorway. In the instant that it catches my eye, I reach out with my left hand – scarcely breaking my stride – scoop it up, and slip it into my pocket.

Turning the figure over in my fingers as I go, I try to work out what it is. Why did I pick it up? A reflex. The way you might take a snack from a plate in passing, even though you're not hungry, or break a switch from a tree, just to have something to tap on the toe of your shoe as you're walking. After a block, I bring it out into the light and look at it. A zookeeper grasping a pitchfork with a large cut of red meat impaled on it. He is wearing grey pants tucked into black galoshes, a mustard pullover, a black tie, a peaked cap. A keeper of the old school, a little chipped and faded.

The whole of the next day, the zookeeper stands on my desk as I'm working, beside the jar of pencils. The desk happens to be covered with green baize, and the little green island he is standing on matches the cloth exactly. It is odd, I think, that he is wearing a tie, in his line of work, although he has also rolled up his sleeves. The meat looks like a bloody comma. An oversized chop, a buffalo chop, fit for a tiger. The zookeeper's head can swivel – it fits into a socket between his shoulders on a tapering peg – and I turn it so that he is gazing at the meat on the end of his fork.

He looks at home among the dictionaries and terminals. And yet he bothers me. What was he doing standing in the wall? A child must have left him there. A boy swinging on the gate, waiting for his dad to come home from work, watching the traffic. I have never seen a child in that funereal yard, but throughout the day a potential boy grows clearer and clearer in my mind, until he is as familiar as the figure itself. I can see this toy in his sticky hand, I can smell the orange he is softening by rolling it between the sole of his foot and the garden path, the better to suck the juice, while his other foot curls on the bottom bar of the gate.

By five, I have decided to take the zookeeper back. I have deadlines to meet and no time for walking, so I drive down to the house in Kitchener, although it is just around the corner. A tricky business. Should I go straight up to the wall and put the thing down? What if someone is watching from behind the windows, which are as blank as dark glasses in the afternoon sun? Should I find some pretext, like pulling up my socks, for returning the toy to its place unnoticed? I park the car in Essex Street and walk back down the hill. For a moment, as I approach the house, I consider dropping the figure in the letterbox, but in the end I simply put it back where I found it, in the hole in the wall, and walk away, half expecting some suspicious voice to call after me.

The zookeeper stands there for a month. Every time I pass, I expect the figure to be gone, but it is always there. Am I the only person who ever looks at this exact spot? Any child going by should notice it. Is this object invisible to everyone but me?

After six weeks, history repeats itself. As I'm passing, my hand rises, involuntarily, and takes the little man from the hole, and puts him in my pocket. He is here now, as I write, flourishing a fresh chunk of meat at me like Tolstoy's punctuation.

the shoes, the socks, the button-down collars, the corduroy jackets. the tables, the chairs. the pavements, the grass on the verges, the flower beds, the impatiens, the Barberton daisies. the street names on the kerbstones, the white lines, the street lights, the bulbs in the sockets. the buckets, the spades. the cars, the caravans, the motorboats. the sheepskin seat covers, the halogen spotlights, the retractable aerials, the loudspeakers, the rubber mats. the driving, the parking, the driving back. the money in the parking meters. the walking in the parks, the drinking in the bars, the talking, the laughing, the eating in the restaurants, the glasses, the wine in the glasses, the knives, the forks, the plates, the food on the plates, the baby potatoes, the stuffed trout, the chocolate mousse, the brandy snifters. the reading, the writing. the paper, the pen, the ink in the pen. the books, the books, the books

59   A table in the Springbok Boarding House, a round table covered with a plastic cloth, in a room with a tall window. There is something lemony about the table. Is it an image on the cloth? The smell of cough mixture? Or perhaps there is a bottle of Rose's lime juice, with limes and their leaves in relief on the glass, a helpful braille for blind tipplers. An old man is sitting at the table, drawing a field of racehorses with numbers on their saddlecloths. Thoroughbreds at the gallop, their muscles tautly sculpted, the fine threads of their manes and tails flying. He is drawing with a blue pen on a lined page from a school exercise book. He is drawing for the child beside him, who kneels on the seat of another chair, leaning forward to see every stroke. There is a jar on the table with a flower in it. The room smells of food, the plastic tablecloth sticks to the child's forearms. A sugar bowl, a wireless, an ashtray. The rest of the room is dim, as if the table stood under a spotlight, but its position in the room is clear: it is in the corner farthest from the door, near the window, and the old man is

facing towards the light. Now he has put aside the horses and is drawing again on a fresh sheet, drawing bicycles, racing bicycles, and the cyclists on them as small and neat as jockeys. The child marvels as the blue wheels take shape, spoke by spoke.

When my grandfather died in the early sixties, this memory was the largest part of my inheritance. The material part was scarcely more substantial: a handful of lapel badges. One of them showed the chevrons of the Citroën marque, another the outline of the African continent on a long pin. All the rest had been issued, at the rate of one a year, by the Railway Recreation Club at Berea Park, where the old man was a member. There were around three dozen of these ornate little enamelled shields, with gilt edges and the initials of the club and year of issue inscribed on scrolls, and not much to distinguish one from another except the dates. But once or twice in the fifties, some creative temperament on the committee had asserted itself (I imagine) and a badge with an unusual shape or colour was produced. There was one in the shape of a fish, coloured the pale sea-green of salmon scales. It must have delighted the club's anglers.

The box in which I kept these badges had belonged to my mother when she was a schoolgirl. It was a wooden casket half the size of a pencil case, decorated with forest scenes made of inlaid segments of stained wood, now faded to a perpetual autumn. There was a secret mechanism for opening the drawer, a wooden switch concealed beneath a small tile that could be slid aside – it fitted so perfectly you could not even insert a fingernail into a crack, you had to moisten the tip of your finger and pull gently. Pressing the switch caused the drawer to spring open.

I liked to spread the badges out, arranging them by shape and colour, or more often by date. The older ones from the thirties and forties had a butterfly stud at the back, but modern jackets did not always have a buttonhole in the lapel and so the more recent badges had pins. My grandfather came to life in these small things, which evoked his hands, resting on the paper and holding the pen. When I grew up, I realized that they were also signs of his belonging in the world, the world of the railway goods yard, the pub, the working-man's club. I imagined him wearing them when he went down to the Berea to watch the football on a Saturday afternoon, or when, on any day of the week, he walked up to the Vic in Paul Kruger Street for a pint. They were badges of identity, simple markers of a life story. The mere gesture of spreading them out, with a casual sweep of the hand, produced a plot. My grandfather's absence during the war years, his time 'up north', was never clearer to me than in the missing chapters in the story told by the badges.

Two boys came to my door one day begging for food, a teenager and his smaller brother, both in rags and looking pitiful. While I was fetching bread and apples from the kitchen, they slipped into my flat and pilfered what they could stuff in their pockets. They did not run away. When I came back with the food they were waiting dejectedly on the doorstep, and they accepted the packet with thanks and quietly withdrew. A day or two passed before I noticed the small absences: a stapler, a travel clock, my grandfather's badges.

Later, I came across the splinters of the box at the foot of an oak in Saunders Street, not far from my home. A few sticks of wood and a rusty spring. Frustrated by their inability to open the box, they had smashed it. Instead of the coins it must have promised when they shook it, the box had coughed up a handful of trinkets. I searched in the roots of the kikuyu on the verge, and scuffed through leaves and litter in the gutter, convinced that something must have been left behind, but whether or not they were disappointed with their haul, they had carried off every last one.

A single badge finally did turn up in my wardrobe, pinned since the previous winter to the lapel of a sports coat. Nothing special, just a variation on a theme: a small gilt shield, with a red banner at the top saying SOUTH AFRICAN RAILWAY RECREATION CLUB and two white banners at the bottom saying PRETORIA and BEREA PARK. In the middle, in gold on a black shield, is a winged wheel and the date, 1951.

Mementoes of District Six is a cabin made of resin blocks. Enclosed ·60
in each block is an object or fragment that the artist Sue
Williamson collected among the ruins of District Six after the
removals: a shard of pottery, a scrap of wallpaper, a hairclip, a
doll's shoe.

'It made me cry like a baby,' says Liz.

'You? Never.'

'Really. I'm no pushover, but it was just so moving, standing
there like a kid in a Wendy house surrounded by these relics,
worthless things made to seem precious, glowing like candles. As
if each trinket and scrap had been a treasure to someone.'

We talk about trifles and their meaning.

After another glass of wine, she decides to show me her most
treasured memento. This is what she would like enclosed in glass
and kept forever. She opens her fingers.

A lucky-packet fish with a breath of her childhood in
its belly.

On the eve of the millennium, South Africa's new police com- ·61
missioner, Jackie Selebi, entered the Brooklyn Police Station in
Pretoria to make an inspection. According to subsequent news
reports, the commissioner was not impressed with what he
found. Incensed by the casual attitude of the charge-office staff
and their failure to recognize him, he called Sergeant Jeanette
Mothiba a 'fucking gorilla'. Sergeant Mothiba responded by
laying a charge of crimen injuria against the commissioner.

The incident was widely reported. Some treated it as a joke
or at worst a blunder. Others felt that the commissioner's language was not just inappropriate, but unforgivably derogatory
and racist. It was an echo of the insulting 'baboon' used so often
by white racists against black people, and all the more shocking
in this instance because a prominent and powerful black man
had used it against a black woman under his authority. One
black female journalist wrote that the phrase conjured up the

image of a gorilla mask of the kind worn at fancy-dress parties, superimposed on a black woman's face. The image would linger, she said, and be used against other black women.

After a fortnight of controversy, the Independent Complaints Directorate, to which the case had been referred, issued a report finding that Commissioner Selebi had not used the word 'gorilla' at all, but the word 'chimpanzee'. This word, unlike the word 'baboon', the report said, was not commonly used as an insult. Although it was safe to assume that the word had been used in an insulting fashion, it was not sufficient to warrant prosecution.

In its front-page report on the Directorate's findings, the *Star* ran an article titled 'What's the difference between a chimpanzee and a gorilla?' The article pointed out that both are anthropoid apes of central West Africa, but whereas the chimp is 'gregarious and intelligent', the gorilla is 'stocky with a short muzzle and coarse dark hair'. The anthropoid apes belong to the order of primates, the article concluded, and so do human beings.

In the end, it was hard to say exactly who the joke was on. Commissioner Selebi, who had started this grotesque drama with his ill-judged comment. Or Sergeant Mothiba, who had vanished behind the headlines. Or the Independent Complaints Directorate, earnestly offering dictionary definitions as a legal defence. Or the reader, poking a stick through the bars at his own beastly nature.

62   In every corner of the library built by Canetti is an idea that could flare up and scorch the passing reader.

Originally, he tells us, laughter was an expression of the pleasure taken in prey or food. This is why we laugh when someone falls. Their vulnerability reminds us that we could spring on them now and tear them apart. Our lips are open, our teeth are bared. But we restrain our animal appetites, and instead of eating, we laugh. 'Laughter is our physical reaction to the escape of potential food.'

A Saturday in July. The air is tinged with wood smoke, clean
sunlight falls on dirty surfaces, bands of sun and shadow laid precisely over man-made crusts of tar and brick, over cement kerbstones, painted black and white, and stencilled with street names.
A sagging fence holds panes of sky in its frayed mesh. Smells of
dust and whitewash rise from the rugby field on the other side
of the fence, reduced to red sand and straw at this time of year.
The edges between light and dark, hot and cold define the
peculiar thrill of a winter morning, when you are out in the
frosted air wearing a warm jacket.

I am standing on the pavement outside the Plaza Pawn
Warehouse in Primrose, delighted to be alive. Minutes ago, on a
set of shelves in a corner, a dead end in a labyrinth of old tables
and chairs, I uncovered a row of books. I had to shift a chair or
two to get to them, and hang over the back of a brown corduroy sofa that smelt of baby food, before my dangling fingers
could pick out a tune on their spines. I chose the book I am
holding in my hand. The cashier, a tubby old man in a pale-blue
pullover, studying the form in a newspaper at a counter behind
wire mesh, seemed surprised that someone would actually buy a
book in his shop, and he was almost embarrassed to charge me
for it. After a moment's hesitation, he asked for fifty cents, and I
counted it out in silver to avoid the further embarrassment of
change. Instead of putting my coins in the till, he dropped them
among some others in a china saucer, a stray piece from a
Beatrix Potter set, dismissing me. Parking-meter money, perhaps, or something for the beggars who come to the door.

The book is *The Pre-Raphaelite Dream* by William Gaunt,
published by the Reprint Society in the early forties. It is not
particularly beautiful and it has seen better days; although the
cloth binding on the covers is emerald green, the spine has been

bleached to khaki by the sun. But that does not bother me, as I did not buy it for its looks. I also have no particular interest in the Pre-Raphaelites. I had to have it purely for its title. Sometimes the name of an author and the title of a book fit one another so perfectly you can scarcely imagine one without the other. William Gaunt, *The Pre-Raphaelite Dream*. It is as familiar as a favourite, a book I have been living with for years.

The encounter with the cashier, feeling the sting of his sublime disdain, and now emerging from the gloom of the shop into the icy sunlight, have made me self-conscious. I become aware of my own incongruity, not just of race and class and language, but of predilection, of need. Far from making me feel uncomfortable, the whole situation pleases me. The sunshine on the tar, which is sugar-frosted with automotive glass from the smash-and-grabs, the Saturday-morning bustle, the East Rand detail – the massive palm near the Plascon paint shop. the Solly Kramer's. a buckled bus shelter. dim-witted robots blinking into the glare. parking meters along Rietfontein Road all ears, absurdly attentive to petty transgression. the yellow stripes on the fascia of Spares Link. the notices about diffs and carbs and shocks scrawled on the window glass in shoewhite. the pink towels behind the burglar-proofing in Top Creations Unisex Hair Salon. the yellow-brick flats above, the potted cactus and caged budgie on the balcony. the women in blankets on the verge across the way, beside their enormous lumpy bags of mielies. Myself in the midst of it, held by the air, with this beautifully inconsequential book, scrounged in a bioscope junk shop, clutched in my hand. I should feel utterly out of place, but instead I feel that I belong here. I am given shape. I do not follow but I conclude, as surely as a non sequitur. It's enough to make me laugh.

The men coming down Thistle Road are laughing too, as if they see my point. Black miners just off shift, wearing helmets with lamps on them pushed back on scarf-wrapped heads, their overalls unbuttoned to the waist despite the chill, their boots unlaced and gaping. Beyond them, against the sky at the end of the road, a church spire. Dutch Reformed is my guess.

I open the book. It was so dark in the shop I could hardly make out the type. The frontispiece is Rossetti's *The Beloved*, captioned with a quotation from the Song of Solomon: 'My beloved is mine and I am his.' The chapter called 'From King Arthur to Karl Marx' turns out to be about William Morris. I flip through the plates: Holman Hunt painting on the shores of the Dead Sea, with his palette in his left hand and a rifle resting in the crook of his elbow; Millais's *Ophelia*; Rossetti's *How They Met Themselves*; designs for stained-glass panels and tapestries by Burne-Jones. Everything in black and white, yet this is not a colourless world. You cannot look at these images without seeing silken red hair, gold thread in an embroidered tunic, the plush blue velvet of a skirt. It all seems more intriguing, with the colour draining into it off the palette of your own memory.

Then I hear a voice raised. A man is teetering on the kerb, haranguing the mineworkers. A young black man, so steeped in last night's booze he can hardly stand. He is wearing a greatcoat many sizes too big for him. He steps down into the street, goes towards the miners and stumbles in among them, shouting words I do not understand, waving his arms and making the tails of his coat flap.

And this makes me even more satisfied with myself. It makes my whole situation more interesting: me standing here, with my irrelevant book, the women on the verge with their mielies for sale, the men in their sweat-stained overalls, made pale by deep-level dust, faces turned to the weekend, the comical drunkard. Together, we are theatre, we are high drama and low comedy.

Then one of the miners takes the drunkard by the collar of his coat and hurls him to the tar. It is an act of such explosive volition that his feet shoot out like a clown's and one slapstick shoe goes flying. You could have knocked him over with a finger and so the blow seems that much heavier. He is not merely tripped up, he is hurled backwards with all the force the other man can muster. He throws him down on the tar as if he is made of an obdurate material he wishes to break. There is a sound like a rock cracking. The miner's companions laugh and come closer, leaving the drunkard lying still in the street.

A car approaches down Thistle. The driver blows his hooter, a pinched white face looks over the steering wheel, demanding that this obstacle be removed.

The miners have stopped to talk to the hawkers. A woman strips the leaves from a mielie cob, exposing a row of white kernels, and hands it to one of the men, and he bows his head to smell it.

64   Here comes a kid with his pants reaching only to mid-calf. From a distance, I think he is wearing hand-me-downs, much too small for him, and feel a pang of sympathy, but when he gets closer I see that he has rolled the bottoms of his pants up to show off his garish sneakers.

Nigel Henderson: 'A new boot is a fine monument to Man – an artefact. A worn out boot traces his image with heroic pathos and takes its part as a universal image-maker in the Suburbs of the Mind.'

65   The house was enormous, made up of five or six bedrooms, a lounge with a fireplace so huge a man could stand upright in it, and a rambling kitchen. A stoep curved around two sides of it and an overgrown courtyard lay at its heart. The two halves of the front door opened inwards like the gates of a castle.

The room I remember best was the smallest in the house, but like all the others it was very tall, so that it seemed grander than it was. The bed was just a mattress on the floor, covered by a floral sheet and a mohair blanket. The height of the ceiling allowed for an immense fall of grey curtain in front of the window. This curtain was the most solid, impenetrable surface in the room, lined with satin and thickly woven, cross-hatched in black and white threads, each as thick as a charcoal stroke. Drawing it would have been superfluous, it was already a study in pencil.

Beside the bed, on a red-polished hearthstone, lay a spill of mysterious objects, communing in delicate shades: yellow gourds, cobs of Indian corn, shells, sand dollars, perlemoen, sheaves of grass, twigs of coral, small unfired ceramic tiles that seemed to have been split from the bed of a dried-up lake. This sun-bleached still life brought the sea into the room. The woman whose room it was smelt like the sea too, especially when she came back from her home at the coast with her hair cut short and her skin burnt brown. In a landlocked city, in a place with no water, I was swept away in the salt tides of her body.

We had lived there for a year when our landlady sold the house to the Apostoliese Geloofsending, who had established a theological seminary next door. Before we even moved out, she brought her salvagers to cart away the details we could do without, the brass plates around the light switches, the cast-iron dados and porcelain door handles. And we had hardly left when they arrived to tear out fireplaces, light fittings and pressed-steel ceilings.

Within the week, the new owners knocked the walls flat and paved the plot for a parking area, as if the lives we lived there had no more substance than a pop song.

I am stripping the bedroom door down to the wood. The paint 66 comes off in layers: layers of taste, of personal preference, of style. I wish I could read these strata the way a forester reads the rings of a felled tree, deciphering the lean seasons, the years of plenty, the catastrophes, the triumphs. Instead, I see nothing but fashion. Nineties ochre, eighties ivory, seventies beige, sixties olive. Paging back into the past.

I am reminded of the Ndebele mural up the road. It is still

there, of course, under a thick, lemon-yellow skin. All summer, after every storm, I have been waiting for it to reappear through the paint, its black edges and angles coming to light again like an old master's pentimenti. But apparently Plascon on plaster does not behave like oil on canvas. To effect this revelation, one would need some paint stripper, a blowlamp, a sharp-edged scraper. Or one of those X-ray cameras they use to hurry on the work of time.

There is an easier way, I suppose. Someone must have photographed that wall. *Style* magazine or the local rag. A dozen kids from the youth hostel around the corner.

But I do not want a photograph.

Sunday morning. The new owner of the house with the secret mural — or perhaps he is just a tenant — is coming down Blenheim Street as I am going up. He is wearing rubber sandals with reptilian soles, satin running shorts, a pair of narrow sunglasses curved like the front end of an expensive car. Under his arm, a folded newspaper; dangling from his hand, a plastic bag full of groceries, the aroma of freshly baked rolls. He slips the bag over his wrist as he unlocks his security gate. I want to tell him what he's missing. I can see myself drawing him back onto the pavement, I can see him gazing at his yellow wall with new eyes. I want to describe the mural, and the man who painted over it.

But I cannot picture this man clearly any more. His work of obliteration hardly took a weekend, and so I couldn't have seen him more than two or three times in all. Now he has vanished behind an impostor. The man I've written down here, the tall one in the overalls, has displaced the one who might have been loitering in my memory. Every time the memory man tries to come from the shadows, this written man, this invention you've already met, steps in front of him. Like a naughty child in a photograph, a Branko, jumping in front of his meeker brother to annoy him, waving his arms, bullying him out of the picture.

Now who's to say whether this painter, this tall man in overalls, was even tall, was even wearing overalls? And who's to say what was in his mind as he finished stirring his paint and stepped back to look at the wall?

A 'pentimento', in the jargon of art historians, is a place where the painter 'repented' or changed his mind, revealed with the passage of time as the concealing paint ages and becomes transparent. In her book *Pentimento*, Lillian Hellman took this process as a metaphor for the writing of a memoir. The appearance of the original conception and the second thought, superimposed within the same frame, is 'a way of seeing and then seeing again'.

There is something to be said for falling back on the fallible memory, the way one falls back on a soft bed at the end of a working day.

This is the version of the painter I will persevere with: he is a sensitive man, not a butcher. It pains him that he has to wipe out this mural, which reminds him of his own past. When he stands in the glow of these colours, he feels the light of childhood on his skin. But he is a pragmatist too, and has to put food on his table. He steps back to look at the wall, to get the whole thing clear in his mind, to let it settle on the damp soil of his memory. He knows that he is the last person who will ever see it like this. Then he takes up his roller and gets on with the job.

In Vienna, at the end of the nineteen-twenties, Elias Canetti   67
befriended a young invalid named Thomas Marek. Marek, who was almost totally paralysed, spent his days in a wagon outside the house at No. 70 Erzbischofgasse, reading a book propped on the pillow beside him and turning the pages with his tongue. He was always intrigued to hear from the able-bodied what it felt like to run, to skip, to jump over hurdles. But what fascinated him most of all was falling. Once, when Canetti tripped and fell in his presence, he was so delighted that the writer resolved to fall again, from time to time, just to amuse him. And he did just that, he says, through the course of their friendship. He became

89

so adept at stumbling and falling 'credibly', without hurting himself, that Marek suggested he should write an essay on the subject, called 'The Art of Falling'. I wish that he had written this essay, I would like to read it.

68   Johannesburg is justly renowned for its scenic waterways. The finest body of water in my part of town is generally held to be the pond at Rhodes Park, established when the city was young on the site of an existing vlei, but I have always preferred Bruma Lake, which replaced the old sewage treatment works on the banks of the Jukskei. When the lake was first excavated in the eighties, as the focal point for a new shopping centre, there were teething troubles: the Jukskei kept washing down garbage and clogging the drainage system. Not long after the grand opening they had to drain the water to make modifications to the filters, and the system has worked well ever since. In 2000 and 2001, when the Bruma serial killers were at work in the eastern suburbs, the bodies of several men were discovered in the water, and the police had the lake drained to search for clues. It was a salutary reminder that the lake was artificial, that it was nothing but a reservoir lined with plastic. There was something fiercely reassuring about that reeking muddy hole in the ground, and it was almost a pity when the frogmen and the waders in gumboots had finished scouring the silty bottom, in vain, and the thing could be filled up with water again.

In Johannesburg, the Venice of the South, the backdrop is always a man-made one. We have planted a forest the birds endorse. For hills, we have mine dumps covered with grass. We do not wait for time and the elements to weather us, we change the scenery ourselves, to suit our moods. Nature is for other people, in other places. We are happy taking the air on the Randburg Waterfront, with its pasteboard wharves and masts, or watching the plastic ducks bob in the stream at Montecasino, or eating our surf 'n turf on Cleopatra's Barge in the middle of Caesar's.

When Bruma Lake was brimming again and the worst of the stench had dispersed, Minky and I had supper down on the quay at Fishermen's Village. Afterwards we took a stroll over the little pedestrian replica of the Golden Gate Bridge, with its stays and cables picked out in lights, and watched the reflections dancing on the dead water.

A schoolgirl turns in from a side street a block away and comes 69 towards me. A little girl of nine or ten, in a Jeppe Prep uniform and short socks, with a satchel on her back. A perfectly ordinary little girl on her way home from school. Or she would be, perfectly ordinary, I mean, if she were not wearing a diving mask and snorkel. Coming towards me, on a spring afternoon in Roberts Avenue, snorkelling through the slanting sunlight.

Assuming that her performance must be for the benefit of spectators like me, for the woman sweeping the stoep at the old-age home or the barber under his canvas awning, I expect her to be giggling or suppressing a giggle. But her face behind the glass is serious. The snorkel tube is transparent, the mask is rimmed with pink rubber, her eyes look out with the astounded, strained expression of a diver who has just sunk below the surface for the first time and discovered a second world. She gazes at me as if I am a fish, a creature covered in spines, trailing poisonous filaments, jagged with exotic colour, and passes me, moving slowly through the air, with bubbles of anxiety breaking around her.

I walk on for a few paces, then glance over my shoulder. She will be looking back to giggle at my bemused reaction, I am sure. Or her skinny shoulders will be shaking, at least. But she is neither looking back nor laughing. She is simply going on, her head drifting slowly from one side to the other, her open palms floating back on the air. There are steps cut into the verge, where the tram used to stop, and she goes slowly down them to the kerb, holding onto the metal railing, puts a foot in the roadway, fords fearlessly out into the traffic on Roberts Avenue.

My feet have turned to lead, my head is round and deaf. She has submerged the world, and me in it. The light streams like water over everything, the grass on the verges shifts in currents of astonishment, as I press on into the deep end of the city.

70   I found *Sunset* by Marios on a Yeoville street corner, left out for the garbage men, along with an illustrated edition of *A Nest of the Gentry* by Turgenev. My first impression – that two more ill-matched objects would be hard to imagine – proved to be superficial. Despite the silken thread of the bookmark and the richly textured, cream-coloured endpapers, the book, produced by the Foreign Languages Publishing House in Moscow in 1951, is poorly designed and printed. The moody theatrical illustrations (by Konstantin Rudakov) would have appealed to Marios. His painting is pure kitsch. It shows a tropical island, with palms and seagulls in silhouette against a sky of layered oils like a complicated cocktail. For many years, I contemplated turning it into an art work by Neil Goedhals. I have the rubber stamp with Goedhals's name, there is an inviting patch of beige beach sand in the foreground waiting for such an imprint, it would be simple. But I always baulked when I saw that meticulously painted 'Marios' coiled like a serpent in the bottom right-hand corner. Now I have given *Sunset* away to the Little Eden charity shop (I've kept the Turgenev). I miss it already. If I didn't have foreign exchange to organize, I would drive out to Edenvale and try to bargain it back.

71   The SPCA book shop in Edenvale is open on Saturday mornings only. Volunteers, nearly always women, sell the books donated to the Society from a ramshackle room adjoining the kennels. Sheep graze in the paddock next to the parking lot,

while a lumbering tortoise scrapes its shell against the fence. Occasionally, a dog will get into the shop and clatter around in a frenzy of delight, sniffng everywhere, bumping into boxes of magazines, dusting the lower shelves with its tail, mad with the scent of ten thousand dog lovers on a million pages. The combination of second-hand books and stray animals is unnerving.

I have employed the Gorilla for some years now, engaging and 72 disengaging it once, twice, a dozen times a day. 'Never leave it off,' my dad warned me. 'Even if you're just popping into the shop to buy a newspaper. It only takes a minute to steal a car.' The action has become second nature. I reach for the lock on the floor beside the seat, hook the pigtail over the rim, lower the arm, clamp the jaws. My mastery is complete. In a few seconds of smoothly habitual movement, I extend my power over my property, laying claim to it in my absence, seizing it in leathery paws with an iron grip; and then I withdraw that power again and reduce it to its proper, meagre dimensions. I can do it in the dark. I could probably do it with one hand tied behind my back. I am a persuasive advertisement for the product and the security it offers.

After an absence of six months, the owner of the bathroom scale 73 is back in the parking lot at the Darras Centre, renting it out to passers-by. To protect the device from wear, he has covered it in bubble wrap secured with packaging tape, leaving a window of clear plastic over the dial.

'How much do I weigh?' asks a scruffy white boy, stepping onto the scale and looking down between his dirty feet.

The proprietor of the weighing stall leans over to look. 'Thirty-two kilos.'

'What does it cost?'

'Fifty cents,' the man says wearily.

'Phew! That much!'

And the boy gets off quickly, grateful that he is not expected to pay.

74   *A letter to my cousin in China* (a film by Henion Han about a Chinese family in Africa)

I Henion and his father travel to the island of Hainan in the South China Sea. Chi Ho Han was born here in the village of Wenchang. As a young man of eighteen he left home to seek work, travelling first to Singapore and then finding work on ships. The Second World War left him stranded in Johannesburg, where he spent most of his life, before emigrating to Los Angeles in 1990. He has been dreaming for nearly sixty years of returning to Hainan, his 'real home'.

But the homecoming is not what he expected. The island has changed, he cannot place friends from his distant childhood or recall the times they shared. The people he meets are equally unsure of him: he cannot explain where he has been or who he is. With the recognition that he does not belong here, that the gap between them will never be bridged, his bewilderment grows. After a day of frustrating questions and half-understood explanations, he is exhausted and confused. Rather than returning him joyfully to the remembered past, the visit has cast him adrift in an uncertain present.

II Henion and his father journey to Taiwan to retrieve the family bones. Henion's mother and grandmother are both buried on the outskirts of Taipei. His father wants to disinter their bones and take them with him to his new home in Los Angeles. And there is something else: he has been diagnosed with cancer. As he prepares for his own death, he wishes to gather the dead around him.

The mother's tomb is easily found. There is a neat slab surfaced with small white tiles, a lettered plaque on the retaining wall, a memorial portrait. Twenty years have stained the wall with lichen and damp, and the portrait is faded and pitted, but the slab is as shiny as a kitchen floor. A workman in a checked shirt and bright red baseball cap breaks off the edges of the slab with a sledgehammer and levers up the panels to expose the coffin. Then he tears away the lid with a pickaxe. Lying on its side within, as if resting on a pillow, is a small skull. This moment of revelation sends the old man reeling. The workman gathers tibia and fibula, rib and scapula and skull, and puts them in a white bag. A denture remains behind in the wet black pulp.

The grandmother's tomb is more difficult. They expect to find a well-tended and orderly cemetery, where it will be a simple matter to identify the tomb, but instead the place is overgrown and neglected, the paths choked by jungle fern and bamboo. They have a photograph showing a tomb with a convex lid, a small white vase at its foot, but even the caretaker does not recognize it. Their search reveals nothing. Then a family friend who attended the funeral arrives to help them, and they find the tomb in the undergrowth, the site marked miraculously by the white vase, standing clean and whole in the tangle of roots and leaves.

III Henion and his sister convey the bones of their mother and grandmother to a crematorium. This is no discreet furnace, where the bones slide politely out of sight and are reduced to ashes behind the scenes. Instead, the cremator scoops handfuls of the bones from a tray into a wok. He squats, in the age-old posture of the artisan, and blazes away at the bones with a blow-torch. In the blue breath of the torch the bones whiten and flake. Is it chance that the cremator and his assistant are costumed so well for their work? From a distance, her blouse has a bony print, all knuckles and vertebrae (from closer up it appears to be writing). He is wearing an abstractly ashen check. They are on close terms not just with the bones, but with the light and the air. Ash and smoke wreathe through the sockets of the skull, fragments of bone and ash are gathered on a sheet of newspaper like crumbs after a meal. There is mortality on the air, they are breathing it in. Bones stand around in basins and tubs, as matter-of-factly as clothes at the laundry or vegetables in the kitchen. The young woman uses tongs and brushes; the hands of the man are bare. The mark of a craftsman. What carpenter would put the unfeeling fabric of a glove between himself and the grain of the wood?

When the heat has made the bones brittle, he smashes them into small pieces. The splintering is unspeakably violent, it makes you aware of the bones in your hands, the teeth in your mouth. The skeleton, especially the skull, preserves the semblance of a unique human form: we can imagine the flesh on this armature. (We know the imaging processes by which forensic scientists – or are they artists? – put flesh and features on the skulls of those who have been dead for years, even for centuries.) So the pulverizing of the skull seems like a long-delayed second death, an obliteration of identity more final than the original burial. The last echo of the physical body fades away. Now even the bones have been reduced to anonymous substance.

The cremator funnels the bones into two funerary urns, gathers the splinters in a pink plastic dustpan. He grinds the fragments smaller with the handle of his hammer, and his assistant flicks the lip of the urn with her brush. Finally, he wraps the urn in a golden cloth. The young woman, with the elegant ease of a magician's assistant, lifts the fourth corner into his grasp. With a practised flourish, a magical sleight of hand, he ties a bow in it. Then he stoops, as if he is going to undo the knot with his teeth or devour something, but the movement is involuntary, a sign of the effort required to pull the knot tight.

IV The final scene of the film: Henion takes a family portrait in Wenchang. We look at these people through the camera, sensing the film-maker standing among us. Thirty villagers are gathered together before a doorway. In the middle, an old man in a white shirt and glasses, whose belonging is uncertain. Someone calls to them: 'You must sit closer together!' Perhaps Henion is making the appropriate gestures with his hands, nudging them into the frame. They shuffle tighter in, closing the spaces between them, absorbing the old man into a collective body. Then Henion appears suddenly in the corner of the camera's eye as he rushes to take the place that has been kept for him in the group.

The camera keeps rolling.

They gaze out, shuffling and commenting, settling down. For a moment they fall silent and solemn, even the babies stop their squalling and gurgling, but as the image fades to black, they burst out laughing. Perhaps it is the laughter of recognition? They recognize themselves as a family, as a community of being, for no other reason than that they are all side by side, contained within a single frame. Or perhaps it is relief? Having held still for the camera, which supposedly immortalizes them, they are released back into life.

GhOsT AlaRm   75
'The Invisible Protector'
Ghost Alarm is a Unique Verbal Alarm System.
By installing Ghost Alarm, even if your property already has an alarm system, you will be safe in the knowledge that should the unwanted happen you will know exactly where in your property the intruder is!
Ghost Alarm is designed and installed specifically for your own premises, covering individual areas and entrances e.g. pool area (child warning)!
Ghost Alarm with the Unique Verbal Warning System will give you enough time to take the appropriate action!
Ghost Alarm is affordable and cost effective (no contract – outright purchase)!
The above are only a few of many features that the Ghost Alarm offers, for more details contact cell 082 963 2019. Free quote/ installation/service.
Reg. Pat. Pending.

A stoep in Good Hope Street. The deep-blue garden walls hold a precise measure of the twilight still. The smell of grass is quenching after a summer day, the dusk lays a cool hand on the back of your neck. We are talking, my friends and I, with our bare feet propped on the wall of the stoep, our cane chairs creaking. We have been talking and laughing for hours, putting our predicaments in their place, finding ways to keep our balance in a tide of change. We could fetch fresh beer glasses from the door of the fridge, but these warm ones, stickily finger-printed and smelling of yeast, suit this satiated conversation better. We speak the same language.

This is our climate. We have grown up in this air, this light, and we grasp it on the skin, where it grasps us. We know this earth, this grass, this polished red stone with the soles of our feet. We will never be ourselves anywhere else. Happier, perhaps, healthier, less burdened, more secure. But we will never be closer to who we are than this.

The women come back from the pool at Jeppe Girls' High with their hair still wet, with the damp outlines of their swimming costumes showing through their cotton dresses. (Sally teaches history at the school and has a key to the gate.) The kids are crunching potato chips from the corner shop. They smell of salt and vinegar and chlorine. The suns of our own childhoods fall on their freckled arms.

'Look!' says Nicky, feigning surprise, as they come up the steps. 'Three drunk men.'

'*Wise* men,' says Chas.

'We've been exploring the limits of our disgruntlement,' I say.

But Dave says that's unfair. I make it sound as if we're going in circles, when in truth we're going forward. And he tells the story about Little Jannie – in Dave's stories the schoolboys are always called 'Little Jannie' – who arrives late for class one morning.

'Why are you late, Jannie?' the teacher wants to know. 'And it better be good.'

'Well, sir, for every two steps I took forward, I went three steps back.'

'Really!' the teacher says with a laugh of triumph. 'Then how did you ever get to school at all?'

'I turned around, sir, and tried to go home.'

Wood's Self Storage consists of five long salmon-coloured build- ings, each comprising two rows of units, back to back, identified by a letter of the alphabet. Each row contains twenty numbered units: a 'unit' is a storage space of 60 square metres, roughly the size of a garage, with a rolling metal door (attributed to the Krazi-Door Company) and a steeply canted roof. The alleys between the rows are paved with interlocking bricks, and the entire complex is surrounded by walls and electrified fences, not the usual stave of strands but elaborately wired constructs as twangy as zithers. The caretaker lives in a bunker on the edge of the property, where several new units are under construction. They cannot keep up with the demand, he says. Our unit is designated as F13.

I like the area. In the shop-soiled veld around these scatter-ings of factories and warehouses you could stumble on the essence of Joburg – if such diffuse, fleeting qualities exist in con-centrate – bursting into the air like the sap of a plant crushed thoughtlessly underfoot. Or it may be wafting less urgently from the spare poetry of the landmarks and the street names here: Rand Airport Road, Simmer and Jack, Refinery Road.

By the time we arrive at Wood's, André and his workers have already unloaded everything into the alley in front of the unit: tables with chairs upturned on them as if it's closing time, shelves, desks, bed, fridge, trunks, boxes. Suitcases stuck with labels to for-gotten destinations. A portrait in a frame, averting its eyes like a bashful café patron. I hate to see my things stacked up in public; but the pavement outside my house was infinitely worse than this semi-private place. A sort of walled community for goods.

Minky and I pick our way through the boxes labelled with thick black Koki. Kitchen – crockery – fragile!!! MS: summer clothes. IV: manuscripts (Missing Persons). MS: study – stationery. But mainly, the boxes say: IV books – MS books – IV books.

'Three or four boxes of books,' says André, 'is normal. Ten or twelve would be unusual, excessive. But this... it's unreasonable, man. If I'd known we were moving a bladdy *library...*'

He's preparing me for the surcharge, and watching the workers sweating under the writing man's burden, I know I won't be in a position to argue.

André has done this a hundred times. He has a special relationship with Wood's – indeed, they recommended him to us. He has cast an eye over our goods, and as extravagant as the quantities of books and papers seem to be, he knows it will all go in.

'Are you sure?' I ask. 'What if it doesn't fit?'

'Please, don't even think about it. I once packed the entire contents of a big double-storey, one of those old Houghton mansions, into a unit like this. They said it couldn't be done. But in the end there was so much space left over we could have set up a ping-pong table in there and played a game.'

So now it's just a question of packing well, of arriving at an elegant, sensible arrangement.

André has a rugby player's moustache, and he's wearing a tiny pair of shorts of the kind you see when they rescreen the Currie Cup finals from the eighties, but he's not the physical type. He messed up his knees (he doesn't say how) and now he can't lift so much as a hatbox. He is a conductor of bearers. He stands in the alley, with the goods ranged around him, facing into the unit, and directs the bearers to one item after another. '*Bring vir my daardie groen tafeltjie daar: sit hom links agter, onder die stoel... Bring vir my nog 'n boks... Bring vir my die groot stoel met die rooi kussing.*' He is constantly appraising the goods out here, scattered on the brick, and the goods in there, stacked in neat and logical configurations, and calculating the balance between the two. Another layer here? A buttress there? He has a sculptor's sense of negative space: he can see at a glance that this coffee table, stood up on end, will fit into the space between those two boxes, with its legs through the back of that chair. He is assembling a huge, three-dimensional puzzle, filling the space methodically and precisely. He must take weight and accessibility into account too. Never so much as scratched a surface, he says, let alone broken something. He is so still when he gives his orders that he appears to have memorized the location of every box, bag and item of furniture. He seldom gestures; a pointing finger would seem like vulgar overstatement. He never raises his voice; all his commands are delivered in the same even, polite tone, so that they seem like the merest suggestions. The workers have absorbed his style, they fetch and carry and stack with the same busy composure, padding softly to and fro, suppressing their groans when they heave up my boxes of dictionaries and manuals, the Uniform Edition of Robert Louis Stevenson, the Complete Works of Joseph Conrad in odds and sods. *'Bring vir my die rottangmandjie … Nog twee groot bokse… Die klein koffertjie: sit hom vir my bo-op die kombuisstoel daar agter… Die suitcase… Die blou trommeltjie.'* The space fills up. I am more and more convinced that it will not fit. But in the end it goes in comfortably. The last few items are slotted in. The computers are stacked on the tall bookshelf on the left, where we will be able to reach them easily when – if – we return; the concertina file of personal papers, the briefcases, the boxes marked 'desk drawers' go under the kitchen table; two standing lamps and a bicycle in the last scrap of floor space, and it's done.

It is surprising to discover that all one's worldly goods can be assembled together in such a confined space. Countless people have more, of course, and countless others have less. But this is a peculiarly satisfying estate: a unit's worth. Perhaps that is the genius of André, the removal man, the great leveller? To ensure that no matter how much one possesses, or how little, it finally amounts to a unit. Neither more nor less. Having accomplished this miracle again, for another grateful client, he tactfully departs.

Now we are alone with ourselves, with this concentrated, material sense of ourselves. *Aardse goedere.* We stand there for a while mesmerized. Then we roll down the metal door and lock it, insert the extra metal clip and bolt it. I put the key in my pocket. We step back and look at our unit, in a row with nineteen others, in a block with four other blocks. It is a filing system. I have put my whole life on file.

While we've been preparing to leave the country, I have been tempted to get rid of things, but Minky has sensibly restrained me. We'll just have to buy them again when – if – we come back, she says. What are we going to sit on if you give away the chairs? You'll need a desk, you'll need a bed. What's the point? And she's right, of course. I would get rid of every useful thing for which I feel no affection and keep a lot of junk we really could live without.

But self storage is a perfect solution. Now I have everything I need, but I do not have to live with it. I am a man of property, but I no longer need to defend it. Everything is contained, everything is contingent. I have created a community of objects, touching one another reassuringly. If ever I need something, I'll simply come here and get it, as easily as a secretary flipping through a filing cabinet. I'll send someone else to fetch it for me. '*Bring vir my . . .*'

In this orderly universe in which everything has a place and nothing can be mislaid, only Fehler's hard and shiny trommel, embedded among my flimsy boxes in the warm interior of the sealed unit, is not at rest. Why did I hold on to this other life? Did I hope to ballast my own record with one that was weightier, more complete? This proximity repulses me.

'We are stories.' It's a notion so simple even a child could understand it. Would that it ended there. But we are stories within stories. Stories within stories within stories. We recede endlessly, framed and reframed, until we are unreadable to ourselves.

78   The plane takes off. I am looking forward to seeing Joburg from the air. It is always surprising to discover how huge and

scintillating the city is, that it is one place, beaded together with lights. As the aircraft lifts you out of it, above it, it becomes, for a moment, comfortingly explicable. Personal connections dissolve, and you read your home from a distance, like one of De Certeau's imperious voyeur-gods. Lionel Abrahams, flying over Joburg by night, saw the 'velvet obliteration' of all his landmarks: 'Everything familiar had been forgiven.' But there is another, more intimate comfort in the vastness: it assures you that someone, inevitably, is looking back. At one of those millions of windows, on one of those thousands of stoeps and street corners, someone must be standing, looking up at the plane, at the small, rising light that is you, tracing your trajectory, following your flight path. But we have hardly lifted into air when the plane banks to the left and the lights dip below the horizon of the window ledge. It is sudden enough to be alarming, this lurch and slide, but I am merely annoyed. I look across the dim sloping interior, but the dull-witted economizer in the window seat opposite has pulled down the shade. Through the other windows I catch the briefest sparkles and flares. The plane continues to bank. We are going to spiral out of here, I can just see it, rising like a leaf in a whirlwind until the entire city has been lost in the darkness below. Disappointment wells up in me, disproportionate and childishly ominous. This failure to see Johannesburg whole, for the last time, will cast a pall over the future. Tears start to my eyes. And then just as suddenly the plane levels out and the city rises in the window, as I knew it would, a web of light on the veld, impossibly vast and unnaturally beautiful.

...

Point B

Reality favours symmetries and slight anachronisms.
Jorge Luis Borges

We make our way to Gate A15. SA 562 to Johannesburg will be boarding in twenty minutes. In a brushcut's yellow nap, the drawstring of a Woolworths tracksuit, a splay-heeled foot in a rubber slipslop, a way of lounging against one another like seals, we recognize our kind. Relieved and repulsed, we slip back into the brown water of South African speech.

André, the removal man, is supervising the retrieval of our possessions from Wood's Self Storage. The van is parked in the alley between the rows of storage units, the workers are moving to and fro under André's instruction. Before a single item finds its way onto the van, he wants everything brought out of the unit and arranged before him, like an orchestra before a conductor. He himself appears distracted – he goes aside to speak on his cellphone several times – but the workers are as calm and unhurried as ever. They carry our furniture and boxes out into the sunshine. It is a relief to see the familiar tables and chairs, it assures us that we are home. Good thing Minky dissuaded me from dumping everything. The only niggle is Louis Fehler's trommel, hot and glossy in the sunlight, throbbing like a guilty conscience.

André starts orchestrating the loading of the van. *'Bring vir my daardie boks… Sit hom daar agter onder die tafel… Bring vir my nog 'n boks.'* These familiar formulas collapse time, drawing the year of our absence into a single pause for breath, an ellipsis.

The phone rings again and he retreats along the alley. Comes back pale, grimacing as he lights a cigarette.

'Is there a problem?'

'It's my sister. She's been missing since yesterday.'

'Jesus, what happened?'

'There was a burglary at her townhouse, the TV and the hi-fi are gone, also the car. But the big problem is the burglars seem to have taken her with them. We haven't heard a thing.'

'That doesn't look good.'

'You telling me.'

The episode overshadows our first night at home. Made insecure by the proximity of our possessions, we speculate about André's sister, quoting the conventional wisdoms about crime scenes and how to deal with them, repeating the platitudes.

A week passes before the body of André's sister is discovered in a field near Cullinan.

Although we hardly know the removal man, we feel caught up in his story. As we feel him to be caught up in ours. He has filed us and retrieved us, weighed our shortcomings and excesses, he knows the way we fit together. Minky phones and leaves our condolences on his voicemail.

In the following days, three suspects are arrested, and then the story comes out in the papers. The two men who killed Estelle Greeff were hired by her husband, Dr Casper Greeff, a Kempton Park dentist. The plan was to cash in her life insurance policies. Elliot Masango and Christopher Njeje overpowered the victim in her house and tied her hands behind her back. Masango then strangled her, after which they wrapped her body in a blanket and bundled it into the boot of her husband's car. They drove to a farm north of Pretoria. When they opened the boot, he was upset (Masango later testified) to find that the woman was still alive. They dragged her out of the boot, and Njeje sawed through her neck with his accomplice's Okapi. It was so painful that she pleaded with them to get it over with.

Passing sentence at Masango's trial a year later, Acting Judge Eben Jordaan said that people may use alarms, high walls and bars on their windows to defend themselves against strangers, but there is no defence against someone you know.

81 Two years after first being put up for auction, the Marymount Nursing Home is bought by the Vroue Federasie. It is to be refurbished as an old-age home. Now I understand why Albemarle Street has been so busy lately, cluttered with shiny

sedans that look as soft as ice cream when it rains. The architects and accountants have arrived.

An unhappy reversal: a place where souls were ushered into the world is now dedicated to ushering them out.

'I had a chat with the developers,' says Mark, 'and they assured me that the old people won't be a problem. Just occasionally one might get out and try to barter a dressing gown or a pair of slippers for a pack of cigarettes. What should we do then, I wanted to know. Oh, just humour them and send them home.'

For years, a panel in the ceiling of my lounge had slowly been caving in. When its collapse seemed imminent, I climbed up on a ladder and tapped some nails into the board. Two considerations made me wield the hammer with restraint: I did not want to dislodge some other part of the ceiling and I did not want to drive a nail through a pipe or cable. Who knew what lay behind? My feeble repairs had no visible effect and the panel continued to sag. Then a gap began to open up between the cornice and the wall. 'One of these days,' Minky said, 'the sky is going to fall on your head, like you-know-who. It's time to call Ben.'

Ben Homan breaks things with the casual ease given only to those who know how to build again. He got up on his own ladder and beat on the ceiling with his fist. The whole thing shook. A volley of nails sprang out of the boards and clattered away under the furniture. He looked down on me. 'It's had it,' he said. 'It'll fall down before Christmas.'

'Just this panel?' I asked hopefully.

'Nah, the whole thing.'

He looked at me with sad, fatalistic eyes.

Somehow I felt that I had to offer an explanation. 'A couple of years ago,' I said carefully, 'the geyser burst while we were away on holiday. Ball valve was shot.' I was mimicking the plumber, trying for the familiar, offhand tone that men use to talk about cars and sports teams. 'The water must have spilled through here and weakened this panel.'

'Nah,' he said, 'it's got nothing to do with that. It's the points of attachment.'

He climbed down off the ladder and with an outstretched arm pointed out the rows of nailheads, in parallels a metre apart, which showed where the ceiling boards were attached to the beams above. 'The joists are too far apart to support the weight of the boards,' he said. 'There must have been pressed steel here before, see. When they took it out and put up boards, they should have put in extra joists. But the builder was probably cutting corners. The ceiling is weak everywhere. It's started on this end, but the whole thing is sagging. You can see it over here.' He took a walking stick from the umbrella stand at the door, the heavy Namibian one with the carved handle, and thumped it against the ceiling. Another bombardment of nails. 'Won't last into the new year.'

I could also see it now, all the boards were sagging gently like the roof of a tent. Why hadn't I noticed it before? It would certainly never look flat to me again. Now that I knew where the *joists* were, I could see too why my emergency repairs had been so ineffective: I had tacked the board painstakingly to the empty air above.

After he'd gone, I picked up the nails. The old ones had a sugar-coating of white paint on their heads; the shiny new ones were my efforts from recent months.

Ben and his assistant Chico tore the ceiling down in a day, unloosing decades of dust and lumps of brick and plaster. Without a ceiling, the room felt strange and bare. The entire house changed shape and function. I spent half the night in the lounge, looking up into the space below the sheeting. I felt the sky pressing down on the roof as if on my own head. The echoing As of the rafters were a reading lesson. Here and there on the rough beams the carpenter's marks were still visible, and the stencilled name of the timber supplier. Pipes and wires snaked over the trusses to the light fixtures and the walls, the corrugated-iron sheets strained under the weight of the night. The removal of the ceiling had exposed the house for what it was, a mere shelter, a pile of bricks and boards propped up on the veld to keep out the elements. Suddenly I was aware not just of the icy air above the iron sheets, but of the musty air below the floorboards, and the damp soil below that. I was suspended, between earth and sky, like an afterthought in brackets.

The next day Ben and Chico covered the floor with tarpaulins and sheets of thick plastic. They spent two whole days building a platform of scaffolding and wooden boards almost as large as the room itself. To save time, Ben said, you have to spend it. Once the platform was in place, they would be able to move freely while they installed the extra joists and the ceiling itself. It would save an enormous amount of time and effort not having to go up and down ladders constantly.

Ben is seventy-five years old. His stolid presence evokes a vanished metaphorical order: as strong as an ox, as placid as a carthorse. He works methodically, precisely and implacably. When he drives in a six-inch nail he uses an eleven-pound hammer, it takes three or four blows, evenly spaced, it goes in straight. He wants to pass these skills on to Chico, who is not yet twenty. Ben thinks of Chico as his apprentice. He speaks to him with unshakeable patience and expects him to work no harder than he does himself.

As he works, Ben talks, in his long-winded, relentless way. Often he tells stories about the other things he has built or repaired – a garden pavilion in Sandton, the kitchen in a house near Sir Edmund Hillary Primary, a roof in Yeoville. He has just finished raising the wall around a house in Norfolk Street. He noticed that there was a jacaranda planted too close to the perimeter and predicted that in a couple of years' time the roots would start pushing the wall over. He could have broken out an arch and put in a lintel, giving the roots room to breathe, but it was costly and the owner said no, he'd rather wait until the wall fell over – if he was even alive to see it – and claim for a new one against the insurance. Well, when it does, Ben told him, give me a ring.

These stories hold me pinned in the doorway of my study. I have work to do, the texts are lying under my desk lamp, lit up like a museum exhibit. But he rolls on like a wagon-wheel or a plough. His stories have no clear beginnings or endings. Like some artful piece of handiwork, one slots seamlessly into the next, so that the opportunity to interrupt is lost.

Occasionally, as if he senses my impatience, Ben talks about the room in a way that is bound to interest me. 'This bit of the chimney is called the *breast*,' he says (and by his intonation makes it sound anatomical). 'You can look it up in your dictionary. Go on. And this bit is the flue. I'm not making that up, I promise. And all the way along the edges here we'll be putting in cornishes. They're under the scaffolding there in the corner, you can take a look. These are six-inch cornishes. The last lot were the four-inch. Too small, cutting corners again. Look it up in your dictionary, see if it's there. Cornish.'

Ben's tools, his scaffolding, his tarpaulins, his overalls are steeped in the work he has done. The smells of wet cement, rusty water, linseed oil, paint, sawdust are in these things. It is months since the new ceiling, as perfectly flat and blank as a new page under a coat of PVA, drove the outside world back to a proper distance, but still the house smells of this specific history of labour.

83 *Hello!* says the slip of paper the man has just handed me. It is the size of a business card and has been cut from a photocopied sheet. BUONA VISTA CAR GUARDS is typewritten across the top. The other side says: I am not a beggar. My name is...... I will watch your car while you are shopping. I am here to ensure your peace of mind and the safety of your property. If you are satisfied with the service, you may offer me a small reward. Have a good day!

'What is your name?'

He takes back the paper, borrows my pen and leans on the

'Do you mind if I take a picture of your keys?' the journalist
from Sweden asks.   84

We are chatting in the garden, under the pagoda tree, and
the bunch is lying on the table between us. The table top is
sprinkled with soft, pale blossoms like tiny dropped handker-
chiefs.

'Not at all.'

She aims the camera, stands up into a better angle, wrings
the lens and presses the shutter. So much for the candid shot,
now for something posed. She jangles the keys at arm's length, as
if shaking water off them, puts them down again near an edge
where the blossoms are thickest. Shifts the foot of a wine glass
into the frame, then out again.

'Such enormous collections of keys! I've never seen anything
like it. In Sweden, only a janitor would need this.'

A tribe of turnkeys.

'I think I've got four keys on my ring at home – and that includes the bicycle lock. You've got dozens here.' She fans them
out with her forefinger, flips over the immobilizer jack for the
car, takes another shot. They shame me now, lying there like the
keys to my psyche, a feeler gauge for every insecurity. 'How do
you keep track of them all?'

The first principle of key management is to separate working groups on interlocking rings. Coming and going through
the front: street-door deadlock, Yale, security gate (outside),
front-door deadlock, Yale. Coming and going through the back:
back-gate padlock, back-door deadlock, Yale, security gate
(inside). Coming and going by car: garage door, car door, steering lock, immobilizer, ignition. Miscellaneous: window lock,
cellar door, postbox.

I have threaded them on to the rings with their profiles
facing in the same direction, like a dressed file of soldiers. Their

noses and chins are familiar to my fingertips, I can find them in the dark.

'Only seventeen, by the way.' I've been totting them up in my head.

'Well, that's not too bad then,' she says.

Genpei Akasegawa's most beautiful sculpture is *A Collection of End Bits of Lead from a Mechanical Pencil*, a small and delicate china bowl containing a frittering of pencil leads, none of them more than five millimetres long. These are the stubs that were too short to be gripped by the mechanism of the propelling pencil with which he draws and so had to be ejected. If you look closely you can see – or imagine – the flat edge at one end and the rounded edge at the other where the lead pressed against the paper, a contour that captures the size of the hand that held the pencil, the strokes it preferred to make, its chosen paths across the page, unique as a brush stroke. What this bowl of leavings represents is time spent, work done, measured against an insignificant deficit.

(Of course, I cannot be sure that this sculpture is evidence of an actual process. It is presented as the accumulated labour of years, but it may have been manufactured in ten minutes, which is all you would need to snap ten cases of unused pencil leads into fragments. I take the artist at his word.)

This sculpture could be a companion to my own *Autobiography*, and that may be a good part of its appeal, for nothing is more pleasing than the echo of one's own voice, even if it is no longer clear which is the voice and which the echo. *Autobiography* is a shallow wooden box resembling a picture frame, containing 392 pencil stubs (at the last count). The pencils that these stubs commemorate were used and sharpened down to nine or ten centimetres, and then inserted in a pencil extender made from a joint of the bamboo that grows outside my window, and used and sharpened again until there was

85

116

nothing left for the sharpener to pare. None of the stubs is more than two and a half centimetres long. If you look through the glass front of the box, the stubs form a layer ten centimetres deep, like the leaves and twigs fallen beneath a tree in the woods. Ten years of tinder. Shake the box and you will see the different colours of the shafts. The six-sided barrel of a pencil lends itself to stripes, and so you will see dog-ends of red and black mainly, the ubiquitous Staedtler, but also blue and gold Faber-Castell and solid green government issue. There is very little lettering left, most of it was scoured off in the sharpening, just here and there an '–astell' or an 'HB' at the chewable end of the stub.

The old man used to sit on the pavement outside the Jumbo. He had a piece of cardboard which he put down on the kerb for the cold, creating the impression that he was fastidious about his ragged clothes. He was a small man with a grizzled white head and beard, made to look even smaller by his oversized army greatcoat. His hands were enormous, good for a man twice his size, and the skin was hard and smooth. I discovered this when I started to give him money. Sometimes, when I put the coins in his hand, my fingertips brushed the skin of his palm. It was leathery, but not folded or creased like a glove. It reminded me of a shoe. The fat pads of his palm, the swollen base of his thumb, the bulging fingers were like the often-polished uppers of old shoes. Why were his hands so big? What work had he done to give them this shape? What substance, grasped or stroked or kneaded over a lifetime, could have given his skin this sheen? It could not be soil. Perhaps it was skin. Is this what skin does to skin?

The cross in the parking lot at the Church of the Holy Angels is

86

117

87 tall enough to challenge the palm tree it stands beside. Our padrão has a shiny metallic frame with panels of blue and white Perspex, lit from within, and glowing in the rush-hour haze at dusk it signals that a bit of Las Vegas has come to Bez Valley. Yet on the whole, the churchyard of this Portuguese parish smacks appropriately of the sea rather than the desert: the white plastered walls offset the colour-coded blues of the roof tiles, the palisades and the notices of the Chubb armed response company.

From the southern side of Kitchener Avenue you can see the blue cross as well as the minaret of the mosque down in the valley, rising above the rooftops like an opened lipstick. The dome of the minaret is exactly the same blue. Was the cross a riposte?

As I'm passing by one day, a priest is coming out of the church. When he sees me, he reaches for a remote control device dangling from his belt like a crucifix and jabs it with his thumb. The security gate someone has inadvertently left open to the pavement trundles shut between us like a curtain drawn in the confessional.

88 We have left the security arrangements for my birthday party until the last minute, resisting the imposition of it, hoping the problem will resolve itself. Once, your responsibilities as host extended no further than food and drink and a bit of mood music; now you must take steps to ensure the safety of your guests and their property.

'I think it's irresponsible of us to have a dinner party at all,' I say to Minky. 'There should be a municipal by-law that only people with long driveways and big dogs are allowed to entertain. We should call the whole thing off.'

'It'll be fine,' she says. 'Just stop obsessing.'

The last time we had people over, I had to keep going outside to check that their cars were still there. It spoilt my evening.

'We'll get a guard,' she says. She phones the armed response people. It is too late, all their guards are booked. But they recommend the Academy of Security, where trainees are registered for on-the-job experience. She phones the Academy. Yes, they do supply security guards for single functions. A dinner party? Sevenish? Can do. That will be the half-shift deal, unless you want him to stay past midnight, and pay the full-shift rate? Being inexperienced, the guard cannot be armed, of course, but he will be under constant supervision. They could arrange an armed guard from another company, probably – but at such short notice, it will be more expensive, you understand? We settle for inexperienced, unarmed, half-shift.

'The security costs more than the food,' I say, 'and he's still an appie. We should have gone to a restaurant.'

The apprentice security guard is called Bongi. So far, he has only acquired the top half of a uniform, a navy-blue tunic that is too short in the sleeve. The checked pants and down-at-heel shoes are clearly his own. By way of equipment, he has a large silver torch and a panic button hanging around his neck. My theory is that he is earning the uniform item by item, as payment or incentive. After six months or so, he'll be fully qualified and fully clothed.

'I knew this was a bad idea,' I say to Minky. 'He's just a kid.'

Bongi is standing under a tree on the far side of the road. He looks vulnerable and lonely. It is starting to drizzle. Minky takes him an umbrella from the stand at the door, the grey and yellow one with the handle in the shape of a toucan, which once belonged to her dad. With this frivolous thing in his hand, Bongi looks even more poorly equipped to cope with the streets.

'This is unforgivable,' I say, 'this is a low point. I'd rather live in a flat than do this.'

'What difference would that make?' says Minky, who always sees through my rhetoric. 'People have still got to park their cars somewhere.'

'A complex, then, I'd rather live in a complex. Some place

with secure parking.'

The guests begin to arrive. Bongi waves the torch around officiously, and then stands on the pavement under the toucan umbrella, embarrassed.

When dinner is served, Minky takes out a plate of food and a cup of coffee. 'Poor kid's starving,' she says when she comes back.

Excusing myself from the table, on the pretext of fetching more wine from the spare room, I sneak outside and gaze at him from the end of the stoep. He's squatting on the kerb, with the plate between his feet on the tar, eating voraciously.

'He's a sitting duck,' I say to Minky in the kitchen, when we're dishing up seconds. 'What the hell is he expected to do if an armed gang tries to steal one of the cars, God forbid. Throw the panic button at them? This whole arrangement is immoral. Especially our part in it. Our friends are insured anyway, if someone steals Branko's car, he'll get another one. What if this kid gets hurt while we're sitting here feeding our faces and moaning about the crime rate? I think he'll have seconds too.'

With a plate of Thai chicken under his belt, and another in prospect, Bongi is looking better. We exchange a few words. He comes from a farm near Marikana, out near the Magaliesberg, and he's been in Joburg since June. His uncle found him this job, his uncle has been a 'full-time security' for five years. He looks quite pleased with himself. Perhaps he's thinking this is not such a bad job after all.

But we cannot see it that way. At ten-thirty, Minky calls him inside to watch the cars from the stoep, over the wall. When the supervisor arrives an hour later, there's a hullabaloo. You've got to maintain standards, he says, especially when you're training these guys. You can't have them getting soft on the job.

That's it, we say to one another afterwards. No more parties. Never again.

In September 1981 it snowed in Johannesburg for the first time in decades. I was working for a mining house in the city. It was company policy that I should sit with my back to the window, to avoid the distractions of blue sky and sunshine, and I might have missed the onset of the snowfall entirely had a colleague in the next office not telephoned and told me to take a look outside.

I tilted the blades of the venetian blinds and watched the flakes sifting down, thinking that it would blow over in a few minutes. One by one, the lighted windows in the surrounding buildings filled with people. Snow falling on Joburg, in spring. It was inconceivable.

At first the snow just speckled the tar and the roofs of the cars in the parking lot in the next block. Then the whole scene whitened. And still it kept falling. People from other departments came into my office, which had one of the better views, giggling and joking. Someone hauled up the blinds so that we could see better, and one of the typists opened a window and caught a few flakes on her palm.

As the snow thickened, you could sense the expectation rising, a wish transmitting itself, binding us into a new community with a single exhilarating thought. Don't let it stop. Let it go on snowing, let it go on until there are drifts in the streets, let's be snowed in, just for once.

Soon the windows in some of the other blocks began to go dark and we saw people coming out into the streets and running around like children let out of school early. But my boss was a stickler for regulations and we had to go back to our desks. By the time we were allowed to leave, just half an hour earlier than usual, six inches of snow had fallen, and it showed no sign of stopping.

The snow changed the city miraculously. We were all in it together. There were traffic jams everywhere, but it didn't matter because they prolonged our time outside. In the streets, white businessmen and black newspaper vendors were throwing snowballs at one another. My double-decker inched its way up Eloff Street. Our bus, our whites-only bus, came under repeated attack from gangs of black snowballers, messengers and cleaners from the office blocks, free to bombard us. They took aim at our windows, so that we would have to open them to clean off the snow if we wanted to restore the view, and then they had a chance to pelt us. After a while some strategist on the upper deck realized that there was snow to be had on the roof of the bus, and, braving a bombardment, leaned out of the window and scraped together enough to fashion a counter-attack. It took an hour and a half to reach the busway on the edge of Joubert Park, where the first snowmen were already standing. But no one minded. Every vehicle had become part of a carnival procession. Every driver, marvelling at the unexpected slipperiness under the wheels, felt out of his element and part of a great experiment.

White kept falling, this cold and foreign substance. People threw colour at one another. 'You want to be white?' the newspaper vendors said, 'Well here it comes. How do you like it?' And the businessmen said, 'You think *you're* white, chucking snowballs at us? Try this for size.' And this 'being white', this 'white' itself, was nothing more than a froth that melted between your fingers or burst apart on a turned shoulder, was something improbable and silly that you could play games with, that did no real harm, that would not last.

Janice and I had an arrangement to meet in Hillbrow. On the bus, I decided that Christmas would come early this year, and so I went into Exclusive's and bought her a book, the Thames & Hudson *Matisse*. It was beyond my means – but the snow had made me generous. I wanted to go through the streets with the brightly wrapped package under my arm like a character in an O. Henry story. We met in the Gattopardo coffee shop and I gave her the book, and she gave me a jersey to put on under my jacket. Then we walked and walked, slipping and sliding like everyone else, clutching at strangers to keep from falling.

In Pretoria Street, outside the Ambassador Hotel, a coloured hobo, barefoot in the snow, took me by the arm and said, 'Don't worry, boss. It's just God defrosting His fridge.'

Louise was in Durban when the snow fell. She drove all the way back just to see it, but by the time she arrived most of it had melted. Within a day or two the city had returned to its cool normality and there was nothing left of the snowfall but a few snowmen, fainting away on the grass in Joubert Park like foolish Europeans who had had too much sun.

The cage occupied by Max the Gorilla has the blatant charm of a garden in Meyerton. There is an expanse of rolling kikuyu and a water feature over on the left. The perimeter wall is good red face-brick covered with greenery (I recognize it as the same creeper I have on my own garden wall, with its yellow flowers and string-bean pods). The gates set into the wall are Windsor green. Here and there, clumps of trees and shrubs have been ringed by fences topped with electrified wires; a sign says that gorillas are destructive creatures and that the new plants must be protected until they can establish themselves. The insulators and strands of wire lend the enclosure a surprising sophistication. What suburban landscape is complete without these things? They are as evocative as river pebbles and railway sleepers. It's as if Max's keepers have set out to cultivate an environment that parodies our own. It is not even a parody. All he needs is a gazebo and a pool, and any one of the spectators would trade places with him.

Max's status as a crime fighter has been acknowledged in many ways. After he was shot, members of the public sent him gifts and donated cash so that a 'burglar-proof' cage could be built for him. He was declared Newsmaker of the Year by the Johannesburg Press Club. Radio 702 sent a man dressed in a gorilla suit to the Milpark Hospital with a message for Max's attacker: We're looking forward to seeing YOU behind bars. Fanie Booysen, a retired zookeeper who had looked after Max for nearly twenty years, came to visit him, and the invalid rose

90

from his sickbed to greet his old friend. The police gave him a bullet-proof vest and tried to recruit him as a reservist.

But the single greatest accolade came when Maxidor, a company that specializes in physical security such as gates and grilles – 'Your home can be the safest place on earth!' – decided to adopt Max. In an official ceremony at the enclosure on 15 April 1999, Max, already embedded in the name of the company and its products, was incorporated into Maxidor as the embodiment of the corporate vision. 'We view our adoption of Max as a long-term relationship. Max will become part of our family as much as we will become part of his. We commit ourselves to be there for him and to support him through anything. With him we will share the growth and changes of life and society in our country.'

If you visit the Johannesburg Zoo, you will find a noticeboard on the viewing platform overlooking Max's cage, where a couple of clippings about his adventures have been pinned up. My American friend is amazed. Where's the merchandise? she wants to know. If Max was an American, there would be a multimedia presentation, a souvenir store, a museum. This would be Max-the-Fucking-Gorilla-World.

91 Piet Retief disarmed me almost from the first word. He had come to my window in the parking lot at Kensington Gardens in Langermann Drive. A sunburnt Afrikaner, with a drinker's complexion under the tan, obviously a tramp, but holding on to his dignity enough to trim his beard and wash his hands. 'How are you, sir?' he asked me.

'Very well thanks,' I said unkindly, 'and how are you?'

'Can't complain.'

Can't complain? *Kannie kla nie*. It was such a peculiar thing for a man in his situation to say. He meant it too, apparently, for there was no sob story and he did not ask for money. We just spoke about this and that, the weather, the fact that the jacarandas make a mess of the pavements. In the end I gave him some small change anyway, with the usual awareness that the first instalment would set the standard for any future transactions there might be, and he accepted it with an air of mild surprise, as if it were my idea entirely, which strictly speaking it was.

There proved to be many continuations. Piet Retief (as I christened him) and I had the same territory. He was a parking-lot specialist. Perhaps he had figured out that someone packing groceries into the boot of a car feels their privilege rather more sharply than an empty-handed pedestrian. So he would pop up in the parking lot at the Darras Centre, or outside Game at Bruma Lake, or around Queen Street, where I had first encountered him. Less often at the Bez Valley Spar or in Derrick Avenue in Cyrildene. He always wanted to have a chat, so that it felt less like begging, I supposed, and more like borrowing a couple of bucks from a mate. Sometimes, if I reached for my wallet too soon, he would carry on speaking as if he couldn't see the money in my hand. And he always pocketed whatever I gave him without looking at it in my presence. In this way we colluded in the fantasy that he was not a beggar.

(Just once, he avoided talking to me. I happened upon him in the toilets at the Darras Centre, in the corner next to Capri hairdressers, washing a shirt in the basin. He pretended that he didn't know me; he threw up a wall of ignorance so impenetrable it made me feel as if I didn't exist.)

The second or third time I saw him, he asked me how the wife was doing. And the kids? I don't have children. He must have mistaken me for someone else, another one of his patrons. But I was in a hurry and so I said, 'Fine, thanks,' and drove off. Probably I was thinking that it was just part of the spiel. What did it matter? He would not be around for long, he would drift away after a few months, the way hoboes do. Let him think whatever he thought. But he stayed. And he never failed to ask after the people at home – *die mense by die huis*. There must have been opportunities to break the pattern, but I let them slip.

'Is the little boy at school yet?' he asked me once.

'Ja, he's in Grade 2 already,' I replied.

I think that was my first actual invention. In time, there was a little girl too. Still at nursery school, cute as a button. It was pleasant having an imaginary family, for a fraction of the effort and expense demanded by the real thing.

Eventually, I acquired a respectable occupation. 'How's the business?' he asked me, out of the blue. 'Pretty good,' I said, 'considering how badly the economy's doing.' 'Ja well,' he said, 'it doesn't matter how bad things get, people still like to swim, hey?' So I went into swimming pools. Later it transpired that I wasn't actually a contractor myself, but a supplier of pool chemicals. Mr Chlorine.

When I told Branko about all this, in a sentimental hour after Christmas lunch at the folks', he was outraged. 'What's your case? Haven't you got relatives of your own? Aren't we good enough for you? You should be ashamed of yourself, lying to this poor sod. Piet Retief... Jesus. If I bump into him – I know exactly who you mean, I've seen him a dozen times and never gave him a cent – I'm going to tell him the truth.'

'You keep out of it,' I said, 'it's none of your business. In any case, half the time I think he was on to me from the beginning. He's invented more of my life story than I have. He's playing games with me, I'm the one you should feel sorry for.'

92 'Kafka,' says Elias Canetti, 'truly lacks any writer's vanity, he never boasts, he cannot boast. He sees himself as small and proceeds in small paces.' Whereas Canetti, by his own account, is ambitious: 'I cannot become modest; too many things burn me; the old solutions are falling apart; nothing has been done yet with the new ones. So I begin, everywhere at once, as if I had a century ahead of me.'

Canetti is also at his best in small paces. Raising an unexpected possibility, asking 'What if?' in a quiet voice: 'A city with secret street-names; policemen tell you where you are if they trust you.' The more ambitious he becomes, the less persuasive he is. *Crowds and Power*, the compulsive enterprise to which he devoted much of his creative energy for a quarter of a century, is his most impressive and least engaging book. It seems always like a monument to a vain cause. For his theory of the crowd to gain the currency of Freud's theory of the individual, people would have to be as interested in their relations to the larger group as they are in the workings of their own psyches. In spite of its significance in the history of the twentieth century, which Canetti set out to grab 'by the throat', and its persistence into the twenty-first, the crowd has begun to seem like an archaic phenomenon. We are becoming fields of disparate beings, according to my friend Leon, the dotcom man, and we no longer need the proximity of others, the press of elbows and shoulders, to confirm our belonging.

Herman Wald's *Leaping Impala* sculpture was installed in Ernest Oppenheimer Park in 1960. Eighteen animals in full flight, a   93
sleigh-ride arc of hoof and horn twenty metres long, a ton and a half of venison in bronze. In the sixties and seventies, fountains splashed the flanks of the stampeding buck, while office workers ate their lunch-time sandwiches on whites-only benches. Although the park deteriorated along with the inner city in the following decades, until it came to be used primarily as a storage depot by hawkers, the herd of impala seemed set to survive the century unscathed. But towards the end of 1999, poachers started carving away at it, lopping heads and legs with blow-torches and hacksaws. At the end of October, a civic-minded hawker, who arrived at the park to find a man stuffing two sev-ered heads into a bag, called the police. They arrested the thief, but he was subsequently deported as an illegal alien and the heads disappeared without trace. A fortnight later, an entire impala was removed from the park by four men, who told secu-rity guards they were transporting it to another park. Stock

thieves. A week after that, another ten heads were lopped. Police later rescued one of these heads from a Boksburg scrap-metal dealer. A leg was found in a pawn shop in the CBD.

Johannesburg has an abundance of wildlife, and the poachers have taken full advantage of the open season. They've bagged a bronze steenbok from Wits University; a horse from outside the library in Sandton (first docking the beast, to see if anyone would mind, and then hacking off its head like Mafiosi); a pair of eagles nesting near the Stock Exchange; and another steenbok in the Botanical Gardens at Emmarentia. This little buck, which had been donated to the Gardens by the sculptor Ernest Ullmann in 1975, was taken in 1998. The head turned up afterwards in a scrapyard and was returned to the scene of the slaughter, where it was mounted on a conical pedestal like a trophy, along with a plaque explaining the circumstances of its loss and recovery. But before long the head was stolen for the second time and now the pedestal is empty.

Of course, urban poachers are not just hungry for horseflesh, any old iron will do. They are especially fond of the covers on manholes and water mains. When Kensington Electrical Suppliers took over Tile City (the cobbler with the goatee had to move on) they painted the covers on their pavement bright yellow to deter thieves, but the logic was flawed: now thieves could spot them from a hundred metres.

Elsewhere in the city, the council has begun to replace the stolen iron covers with blue plastic ones. These bits of plastic tell the scrap-metal thieves to go ahead and help themselves as the authorities have given up on protecting their resources. The council could wrest back the initiative by lifting all the remaining iron at once and selling it off. They could apply the same argument the Botswana government uses for the controlled sale of ivory. Get the jump on the poachers by selling the booty yourself.

The urban poacher is a romantic figure. In unequal cities, where those who have little must survive somehow by preying on those who have more, the poacher scavenging a meal from under the nose of the gamekeeper may be admired for his ingenuity and daring. AbdouMaliq Simone: 'There are young people in Johannesburg who spend twelve and more hours a day simply passing through different neighbourhoods, different parts of the city, seeing what can be taken easily, but also running into others like themselves, who pass along information and impressions, sometimes teaming up to do "jobs", sometimes steering each other in the wrong direction.'

Colour is not the strong point of Kensington Electrical Suppliers. The proprietors painted the building charcoal in an effort to discourage graffiti, but it served as a very effective ground for certain colour schemes and before long the walls were splashed with drawings again. After enduring the insult for a couple of years, they painted over all the graffiti and added a sign: THESE PREMISES ARE UNDER 24-HOUR SURVEILLANCE. Is that really a camera? A rickety contraption has been suspended from the gutter, a Heath Robinson scarecrow.

Chas is halfway across the garden, fishing in the pocket of his pants for the key of the cottage, before he sees the burglar on the window ledge, silhouetted against the sunroom panes, caught in the act. The dramatic backlighting of yellow squares on a black grid, the looming, foreshortened figure, arms and legs spread to brace himself against the glass; afterwards, when he tells the story, Chas will be reminded of a Soviet poster depicting the rise of the proletariat.

94

(The sunroom is a soft spot, everyone says so, including the man who installs security gates.)

For a moment they both stand frozen, and then the burglar leaps down and rushes at him, raising a knife in his hand. Chas trips and falls back on the lawn beneath the washing line, and the man stoops over him, shoulders hunched, slashing the air in front of his face. This ostentatious calligraphy still hovers, luminous and pulsing, preventing Chas from stirring as effectively as if he had been pinned to the earth by the blade, even after the knifeman withdraws, which he does slowly, when no resistance is offered, with a nonplussed air, towards the garden wall.

(Another soft spot, everyone says, lapsing into the technical language of security, the wall isn't high enough, the perimeter can be breached.)

On top of the wall the burglar pauses, as if he has forgotten what he is doing here, and calls down:

'What time is it?'

'Half past seven,' Chas guesses, and these ordinary words stick to the roof of his mouth.

With a satisfied grunt, the man jumps down into the street.

Later, beneath the arrowheads of arum leaves, we find the monkey wrench the burglar dropped, a chunk of rusted iron as long as his arm, weighing all of three kilograms, with a jaw that can stretch to ten centimetres. A hyperbolic restatement of something useful. We keep it beside the fireplace, less as a trophy than a measure of everyday abnormality.

95   A guard is waiting for us at the end of the row of parked cars, semaphoring with his torch. We coast down the avenue towards him, over a familiar surface of wet tar, pushed up into humps and ridges by the roots of the trees, acorns crunching under the tyres. He directs me into a parking place and then retreats to a well-trained, discreet distance. His uniform is black, almost military, with a leather bandolier over his shoulder, combat boots, regimental flashes on the sleeves. There was a shower earlier and the air still smells of wet earth and trimmed foliage. On the garden wall, the ivy has been trained along a lattice of wires to form diamond patterns against the white plaster. I pull the little lever next to the seat to open the boot, and Minky gets out to fetch the present and the bottle of wine, while I engage the Gorilla.

'Good evening, sir,' says the guard as I join Minky on the

pavement. 'My name is Sifiso and I'll be looking after your car this evening. Johnson will show you the way.' He casts the beam of the torch on his colleague, waiting twenty metres away. I see that Johnson has a pistol on his hip. Top Flight Security: We mean business.

'Damn, I forgot to take the price off the wine,' Minky says.

'Give it here. You'll break a nail.'

We go along the pavement towards Johnson, who is smiling genially. I scratch at the sticky tag with my thumbnail.

'Should I give them something?'

'When we go.'

'If the car's still here.'

'Exactly.'

An enormous drop of water explodes against the lens of my glasses.

'Good evening, sir. Good evening, madam.' He unlocks the wrought-iron gate, ushers us through, locks the gate again behind us. Then he leads us up the driveway, shining the torch backwards, expertly. 'Watch your step, it's slippery here.' Minky, who is wearing heels for the occasion, takes my arm. The beam slides over bricks, leaves, the shiny toes of our shoes.

At the end of the drive, there is a gap in the creeper-clad wall. He passes through that and stands aside. 'It's not this door here, but that one over there, in the white wall. Just follow the path. Enjoy the party.'

There is music on the air, laughter, talk. The path is a string of slate islands in a glistening sea of lawn. We go along it, hand in hand, towards the murmur of hidden voices.

Laden with groceries, I push open the door from the garage into the garden with my foot and take two steps along the back path.   96 Stop dead as a stranger appears at the corner of the house. My height more or less, my age, neatly dressed in a leather jacket, jeans, three or four days' stubble on his cheeks.

131

Before I can speak, he points urgently to the garden wall and says: *'Soontoe!'* That way! as if I am late for an important appointment or he wants to get me out of harm's way. I look at the wall, which is blank, I look at him. He is earnest, healthy, tense. I can see the ball of his fist in his jacket pocket.

'Wat maak jy hier?'

'Daar was 'n dief, baas.'

It is mid-morning, sunlight pools like oil on the black leather, the garden is damp but the clouds have lifted. I feel my heart beating near my collarbone, but I am not afraid. We are having a reasonable conversation, chatting like neighbours. If my neighbours called me *baas.*

'What do you mean: There was a thief?'

'A tsotsi was stealing here. I am chasing him away.'

He gestures again towards the wall. Now I understand: the thief went that way.

'I find that hard to believe.' My tone is more than civil, it is stuffy, schoolmasterly. 'But thanks all the same.'

'I have saved everything.'

'Yes, thank you very much. And now you should be going.'

We need to keep up this pretence. If we can go on lying to one another, and more importantly, believing one another, everything will be fine. Neither of us will have to do what the situation demands of him. I should drop the groceries and run out into the street, yelling for help. He should point a gun at me. Does he have one?

'The door is over there.'

He goes up the steps to the stoep. We are still talking about tsotsis, about how bad they are, and how it is a good thing to chase them and save everything. I follow him at a distance, there's really no rush, across the stoep, down the front path to the street door. He cannot open the catch. I put the shopping bags down and he stands aside so that I can open it for him. *'Seblief baas, dankie baas.* Remembering his pleases and thank yous. He goes out.

The instant the door shuts between us, the pretence falls

away. He runs down the road and I run into the house. There are goods scattered in the lounge, clothes, hi-fi equipment trailing cables, there are splashes of blood in the hallway. The fiction that the thief and I have just spun together bamboozles me: it must be the blood of the tsotsi who went over the wall. Caught red-handed. Tangled in this story, I follow the trail into the kitchen. Stop dead as another stranger turns towards me. He is in the corner behind the Morris chair, against the windows, where I cannot see him properly.

Hemmed in here, with my possessions stacked on the kitchen table and blood on the floor, there is no room for pretence. My skin turns to parchment, the wires in my joints snap. He lets out a startled cry. There is no drama, only ballet, a fear-filled pas de deux. He springs out from behind the chair, brandishing some-thing in his hand, and rushes at me. We grapple and fall, I'm trying to fend off his hand, I cannot see what's in it, we tumble over one another until he thrusts me away and I rattle sideways, try to get to my feet and stand on something slippery – it is Minky's silk shirt, her blue silk shirt – half fall under the kitchen table, scramble up again to my knees, knocking over a chair. If he had a knife, he would have plunged it into me, surely, he would have run out of the front door, but instead he has leapt back behind the Morris chair and crouched down. I crouch behind the table. We gaze at one another like two cornered animals.

Then my legs begin to work, I stand up and back out, and close the door, try to lock it, find that the lock is broken. The threshold smells of the thief, as rank as if a cat had sprayed against the doorpost. Perhaps he has pissed himself.

The Flying Squad's number is taped to the telephone table. I dial it, begin speaking in gasps, realize I have reached an answer-ing machine: *Please be patient. Your call will be answered.* I drop the instrument and run back to the door, try the lock again with trembling fingers, but it won't engage. Bloody palmprints on the frame. I drag an armchair in front of the door, run back to the telephone.

A person now.

'I want to report. a burglary.'

'Is the burglary in progress, sir?'

'One of them. is in the kitchen. The other one. has run away.'

'Are they still there? Is the burglary *in progress?*'

I see the thief stumbling across the lawn below the window. How stupid of me! The front door was locked when I came in, so they must have broken in through the back. He must have cut himself on the kitchen window. The first guy steered me away from that corner to give his accomplice time to escape. But why has it taken him so long? He's been crouching there in terror, that's why. He's as scared as I am.

There is a walking stick in the umbrella stand at the door, which Minky brought back from Namibia, a heavy thing with a carved handle. I grab it and run outside. The thief is struggling to get up on the garden wall. It is high here, and after the monkey-wrench man we made it even higher, with metal palisades and spikes. He is scarcely more than a teenager, slight, with a yellow canvas hat on his head, a silly round kwaito hat like a toddler's. He sees me coming, keeps on scrabbling against the surface of the wall. I hit him. He wards off the blow with a raised arm, yelps, scrambles into the shrubbery. He has a bloody shirt wrapped around his right hand, it is my shirt. I hit him again. The stick glances off his shoulder and the carved knob jams among vines and trellises. While I'm trying to work it free, he gets up on the wall, straddles the palisades. I leave the stick and grab the cuff of his trousers, pinning his leg between the slats. He plunges over, one tackie goes flying, I hear him thump down on the pavement outside.

He will go down the hill to Bez Valley like his pal. I retrieve the stick, run to the garage, fling up the door. There he is on the opposite pavement, limping in his bare foot. I am going to beat the living daylights out of him.

No, I have gone too far. It's like this: I see the thief crossing the lawn below the window. I grab the stick from the stand at the door and rush outside. He is on top of the wall, straddling the palisades. I wave the stick at him and he plunges over.

And even this is too far.

The story is going around that burglars use a secret language of litter to mark houses where there are easy pickings. In this code, a red Coca-Cola bottle top means a place is poorly defended: there is garden furniture to be had, the windows at the back are not burglar-proofed, the BEWARE OF THE DOG sign on the gate was left behind by a previous tenant. Whereas if the place is flagged with white, say a scrap of plastic caught on an acacia thorn at the back gate, you'd better watch your step: there are sensors in the garden, the old lady has a gun.

'The police say there's no truth in it,' I tell Branko. 'But residents are advised to keep the pavements outside their homes clean and tidy anyway to discourage loiterers and petty criminals.'

My brother snorts into his macchiato.

'It's hard to imagine how such a code would work in Troyeville,' I go on. 'There's so much crap in the streets, you'd have to be an expert to decipher it. What do they call them?'

'Garbologists.'

'That's it. Maybe this rumour was started by one of the garbologists at Pikitup. Part of their economy drive.'

Branko perks up, I don't know whether it's the coffee or the conversation. 'Interesting notion, that every rumour goes back to an original source, that there's a Typhoid Mary at the root of every cockamamie urban legend.'

'It would be someone like you,' I say. 'Someone obsessed with litterbugs.'

'You can scoff,' he says, 'but you'd be a different person if you moved out here. It's so much more agreeable. You should try it.'

We are having coffee at Sandton Square. This is our third venue since my brother moved north. We tried the Europa in Norwood, but you couldn't hear yourself think with the traffic noise, and the Brazilian in Rivonia Road felt like a cheap imitation, even though it had a conveyor belt.

'There's a unit going in the complex.'

'God forbid.'

'It's a prime site, very private, and not too close to the wall.'

'I would die out here,' I say. 'I need the buzz.'

'I thought writers needed peace and quiet.'

'Not everyone wants earplugs. Dickens couldn't work without the noisy rhythm of London outside his window.'

'Dickens again. Christ, I wish you'd read some Mayhew instead. Better yet, some Auster or some DeLillo. We're already in the twenty-first century and you're still harking after charabancs and gaslight. Get with it, man. The clock's ticked over and you're *two* centuries behind the times.'

98   He rattles the metal catch on the back gate every third or fourth day. When I lift the curtain at the bedroom window to see who's there, he shows his face between the iron bars of the gate like an identity card. He used to say his name, but now he has fallen back on this visual shorthand. Even in the gloom, I recognize his white peaked cap. I go out and let the money fall into his cupped palm. He squints at me through the bars and drops a little curtsey. Neither of us says a word. We have been reduced to a simple mechanism of supply and demand. Occasionally, I spy on him as he leaves, counting the coins, stepping out quite confidently. I think he is pretending to be a backward rustic to keep my sympathy.

'Hello.'

99   'Glynis here. Listen, what's the name of your security company again?'

'It's N.I.S.S. What's up?'

'Have you got their number?'

'I've got the emergency number here, there's a separate one for admin. Are you thinking of joining?'

'I'll look it up in the book. N.I.S.S.? Sorry, can't chat.'

And she hangs up.

A week later, she phones to apologize. She was in a bit of a flap, she says. The neighbour's charlady had overheard some dodgy characters plotting to burgle her house and came to warn her. Panic stations. All she could think of was getting a security company, fast. N.I.S.S. arrived within the hour to put up their signs, although they were really busy and could only install the alarm a few days later. In the meantime, they promised to send a patrol car around from time to time. Still, she hardly slept a wink until the alarm was put in.

'And how's that working out?'

'Bit of a relief. At least we don't feel we have to defend our property with our bare hands any more. On the other hand, it keeps going off for no reason and scaring the hell out of us. N.I.S.S. says it's the cats or the fridge or something. Teething troubles.'

Despite the alarm, Glynis is jittery. She wants to put her house on the market, but Sean talks her out of it. 'Everyone keeps saying Troyeville's going downhill,' he says. 'What are they talking about? It's always been at the bottom of the fucking hill. Just think about it for a minute. It was fucked when I was a kid, in an Afrikaans sort of way. It was fucked when I was a teenager, in a more Portuguese sort of way. And now here I am, fully grown, surrounded by Angolans and Nigerians – and guess what, it's still fucked. It's just a different shade of fucked.'

I remember: one Saturday in the eighties, it must have been, Liz and I were walking in Troyeville. We passed some row houses in Nourse Street that appeared to be empty. There was no gate, so we went onto the stoep of one place and peered through the window, cupping our hands over our eyes to shade the glass. In the middle of the room looking back at us was a tiny man with long dirty hair hanging down from under a Stetson, wearing denim jeans tucked into cowboy boots, holding a knife in his left hand. The knife seemed disproportionately large, like a pantomime dagger, but only because the man himself was so small, almost a midget. Scarcely had our eyes picked out the figure in the gloom, had our minds acknowledged what our eyes perceived, than the little cowpoke burst through the front door, rabid and enraged, cursing and raving in Portuguese, spraying spittle, flourishing the knife. We scrambled to the pavement, falling over one another, and fled back to Yeoville where we felt safe.

100   The house was run-down, set too close to the street on a busy corner and overlooked by blocks of flats. It was the sort of place you would expect to be rented out cheaply to students. We lived in it for six months with our foam mattresses and vinyl beanbags, bookshelves of brick and board, overflowing ashtrays and dog-eared paperbacks. We were white kids from middle-class and professional homes. To obscure the extent of our privilege, we were obliged to practise carelessness and cultivate squalor.

The best thing about the property was its garden. A profusion of shrubs and creepers and flowers made a soft green island in which the house nestled, cut off from the concrete and glass of Berea. You could sit out there on a rickety bench and imagine you were in the countryside or the suburbs. The noise from the traffic was filtered to a muffled rumble through leaf and stem and green shadow. It was a garden that resisted what little maintenance we were inclined to offer. It simply grew and overgrew and fed on itself. To enjoy it, you waded through grass or forced a path in the undergrowth to a place where you could sit and smoke and talk.

A man lived in the room at the back. He came with the house, and our lease with the agent stipulated that he could not be evicted. Presumably he had been abandoned there by the owner to keep an eye on things. A caretaker. We hardly ever saw him. During the week he worked long hours at the General Hospital as a cleaner; on weekends he stayed in his room and drank. From time to time you would see him weaving in with a plastic bag from Solly Kramer's.

After we had lived in this house for four or five months, we had a party. The following morning, as Ivor and Dave and I cleared away the debris, it occurred to one of us that the caretaker might want the leftover liquor, a few bottles of dubious spirits and a five-litre flask of Kellerprinz that was three quarters full. Roma White, bottled heartburn.

The caretaker was in his room. He came round to the side of the house, to the small stoep that opened off the lounge, where the ruins of the bar stood, a trestle table full of greasy paper plates and bottles. He was in his underpants, still a little drunk from the night before, his eyes unfocused. We gave him the Kellerprinz. It was an archetypal exchange.

He squatted at our feet in the sunshine. He was a parody of a servile tribesman in the presence of white authority, desperate and abject; and we were parodies of white authority, middle-class kids in scruffy clothes, well fed and embarrassed. He stuck his forefinger through the eye on the neck of the bottle, pressed its mouth to his own and tilted its fat belly up on the length of his forearm. He drank until the bottle was empty. He drank it down in one gulping flow, as if we might change our minds at any moment or had asked him to return the empty bottle immediately. I had never seen anything like it. He poured the wine into himself as if through a funnel, like a man quenching a fire, or rather fuelling one, stoking something in his tissues that dare not burn out. I had been taught that holding your liquor was one of the manly accomplishments. I was filled with appalled admiration.

When he had drained the bottle he lowered it to the ground and sat there dazed. Several times he tried to rise, but the weight of the bottle kept him anchored. His knees would unfold him as far as the length of his arm allowed, before he dropped back onto his haunches. He went up and down like a pump. Ivor and I disengaged his finger from the eye. Then we each took an arm and steered him towards his room. There was nothing to him, he felt like a husk, and I fancied I could hear the booze sloshing inside him.

His room faced the courtyard where we sometimes sat in the mornings, eating our Jungle Oats, smoking the first cigarette of the day, feeling that we were in charge of our own destinies. In there it was dank as a well. A flare of soot in one whitewashed corner showed where a Primus stove had given up the ghost. There was none of the comforting clutter of servants' rooms. You looked in vain for a newspaper-lined tea chest, a scuffed suitcase, a zinc bath – those familiar objects that let you press your conscience to the warm memory of a nanny's back.

In the middle of the room was a bed. Not an ordinary bed raised up on bricks, but a hospital bed with a black metal frame that could be tilted up at either end, with winches and slings and pulleys for splints and traction and burns, and rubber wheels on the ends of its long legs. The bed was wide and high, and it threw the small room out of scale, dragging down the ceiling and pulling the walls closer.

We took the caretaker as far as his door. Astonishingly he could still walk by himself and haul himself onto the mattress. The bed was tilted up at the head and the foot. He lay down in this obtuse angle on his back. When we looked in that evening he hadn't moved. He was lying there cracked, folded in half like a banknote in a wallet. But the next morning when we looked in again, half expecting to find him dead, he had gone to work.

In the end, he repaid us handsomely for all our kindness. Four of us came home from university one afternoon to find that he had tidied away the garden. It was gone. He had up-rooted everything it would not have taken an axe to fell.

We sat outside in Dave's Volksie for a long time, looking in disbelief at the bare earth, raked smooth from fence to fence, and the pile of dead plants as high as the roof. We laughed and laughed, but it did no good. The house was ruined. Without the garden it looked ugly and unloved. It was obvious that we would have to move.

Tammy is sitting at J.B. Rivers in the Hyde Park shopping centre on a Friday afternoon, drinking a glass of dry white wine, waiting for her husband Joshua. They are going to see *The Truman Show* at last. She is eavesdropping on the tables near her: some white twenty-somethings on one side, making holiday plans, and some black twenty-somethings on the other, discussing property prices and unit trusts.

Tammy has the journalist's habit of seeing feature articles everywhere. She whiles away the time composing an arresting opening line: 'Gold always looks better on brown skin.' Crude. Rather: 'There is a certain kind of chunky gold jewellery that looks better on brown skin.' Another angle: 'The yuppies and buppies might not be sharing tables yet in the happy hour at Hyde Park, but they do share the chunky dah dah watches and strappy blah blah sandals.' She really ought to brush up on her branding. The right labels lend a knowing sophistication to this kind of piece. She's always busking, looking things up in *Elle* or asking Josh, it's always second-hand. After the movie, she should do some window-shopping for designer colour.

As she's turning the phrases over in her head, chunky this, strappy that – Blahnik, that's what she was thinking – she fingers the rosary of her keys. Front door… security gate… bedroom door… and comes to a key she's never seen before. An odd-looking key with a black loop and a thin brass stem. In addition to the standard bit it has a small blade like a skeg sticking out at right angles on one side. It looks less like the key of a house or a car than something you would use to arm a bomb. For the life of her, she cannot identify it. The immobilizer is on a special ring. The postbox is this one…

She is still puzzling over it when Josh arrives. He glances at it, says it's probably something at her mother's place – she's got the spares to her mom's townhouse – and then he hurries her off to the Metro. He always makes her sit through the ads, tells her to pay attention.

All through *The Truman Show* Tammy is thinking about the key. She knows it's not her mother's, she keeps those separate. But the next afternoon she drives over to Craighall Park anyway. Her mother doesn't recognize the key either. They try it in the obvious places, they check it against her mother's bunch, they even get out the spare keys in the old cutlery tray in the kitchen dresser. No match.

A few months later, Minky and I are introduced to Tammy and Joshua at a dinner party. Over dessert, Tammy tells this story. Then she takes out her bunch and shows us the mysterious black key. Her keys are passed around the table. At first, there are tipsy jokes about alien abductions and love nests, but soon the conversation turns serious. It's an unsettling idea, already people are fidgeting in their pockets, where their own keys are beginning to weigh more heavily.

We offer logical explanations. The most persuasive, I think, is Leon's. He says someone at the garage must have put the key on her bunch the last time the car was in for a service; perhaps they parked the car outside in the street and used a security device of some kind, and then forgot to remove the key afterwards. She should call them up and ask. Or it might have been a careless locksmith. When last did she have a key cut?

A woman whose name I've forgotten, a therapist apparently, says it's obvious Tammy put the key on the ring herself and knows exactly what it's for, but is repressing this knowledge. It must be something unpleasant. Does she have a gun-safe? the therapist asks. She has one herself and the key is weird. She takes out her own bunch and shows it to us.

This theory doesn't win much support. But there are a few takers for the idea that the thing is a hoax. Someone's playing a joke on her. A colleague at the paper perhaps? Dave suggests that someone might have put it there with a more serious purpose, to provoke some thought about security. Or rather insecurity. Less a practical joke than an object lesson. By then half of us have our keys out and are picking over them. Even Liz, who's been laughing the whole thing off, fetches a bunch from her handbag in the lounge, which proves to be bigger than anyone else's, and names them one by one, looking distractedly at their profiles as if they are the members of an extended family.

On the way home, Minky says she thinks Tammy has made the whole thing up. It's some sort of party game. That bizarre moment, when everyone stopped talking and just sat there, hunched over the table, picking through their keys in the candlelight... She'll write an article about us. You watch.

'A week ago,' Lesley says, 'someone dumped a pile of rubbish on the pavement in Bezuidenhout Street. If it was a small pile, I would swallow my pride, go out there with a bag and clean it up. But you'd need a bakkie to take it away. It's too big for one person to manage. Now it's come to the notice of everyone looking for a place to drop their shit. So the pile keeps growing.'

Supper on the back stoep of her house in Ellis Street. A cool, clear sky through the vine leaves of the pergola, a warming yellow light from the open doors of the lounge, from buttercup walls dotted with Amnesty prints in black and white, and Ndebele beadwork in full colour. On the table, summer-squash soup from the vegetable patch. Earlier we browsed through the herb garden, picking leaves to crush under our noses, and those sweet-and-sour juices are still on our fingertips. Lemon thyme, marjoram, mint. The sage in the butter sauce came from the garden too.

This is a farewell dinner.

'You're the last person I thought would emigrate,' Minky says. 'You've always been such a... South African.'

'It's time,' she answers with a laugh. 'Signs and omens, things unplugging themselves, cutting me off. The TV is broken. My cellphone has been stolen. Two nights ago someone broke into the shed and stole the gardening tools.'

The ties to people and places, the bonds of work, friendship, conviction we thought would have to be hacked through with a will, have loosened too. The writing, the photography, the film-making on working people, colonial history, Aids, the political work, the teaching, the activism, none of it can hold her. She no longer believes she can make a difference; or rather, she no longer believes in the difference she can make. She has lost faith, she is afraid of living alone, of growing old in this violent city.

Under the carport, against the wall of the house, stands a row of seedlings in small pots. She gives us a chilli plant and instructions on how to care for it. Now we know what this evening will taste like in years to come. As we drive back to Troyeville, Minky holds the plant on her lap, a pale sprig sticking up out of the damp soil, with two curved leaves like the flukes of an anchor.

103 As it turned out, Isaac Mofokeng, the man who shot Max the Gorilla, was no lovable buffoon, he was a violent rapist. Earlier in July, before his encounter with Max turned both of them into media celebrities, he broke into a Johannesburg house where a young woman and her boyfriend were relaxing after a shower. He abducted the couple at gunpoint and drove them to Soweto, where he locked the man in the boot of the car and raped the woman in a field. When he was brought to trial, the charge of malicious damage to property arising from the shooting at the Zoo paled beside the other charges of robbery and rape. Just a week before Max was adopted by Maxidor, the Johannesburg Regional Court sentenced Mofokeng to forty years in jail.

The caged man, the one who paces up and down outside the

Gem Supermarket like a creature in captivity, begs from time to
time, in an offhand way, as if it does not really matter to him.
He'll beg for a while, breaking off his walking to ask for money
in a low voice, and then he becomes more and more engrossed
in his own rhythm, carried away by it, until he stops accosting
people altogether.

One Sunday morning, I was spying on him when he asked a
young couple for money, and the woman emptied the change
from her purse into his palm. He examined her offering curi-
ously. Before she could walk off, he began to pick through it
and give the smaller denominations back to her. After a
moment's puzzlement, she held out her hand to accept the
rejects. She seemed fascinated by the exchange: his raw fingers
picking the coppers out of the pile and laying them on her soft
white palm, occasionally dropping a ten- or twenty-cent piece
that took his fancy in the breast pocket of his shirt. I imagine
that he would have winnowed the entire handful, but the
woman's companion, who had been edging impatiently towards
his car at the kerb, suddenly realized how improper it was, how
ungrateful and insulting, strode back, struck the caged man's
wrist so that coins flew everywhere, grabbed her arm and hur-
ried her away.

Ag no, it's Piet Retief. I've come up behind him on Kitchener
Avenue in the late afternoon, labouring along towards the
Darras with all his possessions slung over his shoulders in two
enormous shopping bags. I could cross the street to avoid him,
but surely it won't be necessary, he'll never keep up with me, not
with those bags. So I just greet him as I pass and pick up my
pace a little, meaning to leave him behind as quickly as possible.
He lengthens his stride at once and falls in beside me, asking as
always about the wife and kids. I offer a few brusque replies and
step out even faster, but still he matches me, heaving the bags up
on his shoulders every few metres. I cannot shake him. After two

blocks I relent. No point in killing myself.

'Where've you been?' I'm not used to seeing him so far from his base at the Darras.

'No, I've been to the bioscope by the Carlton. Do you know it?'

'The Kine Centre?'

'Ja. For seven rand fifty you can watch films all day. Only at six everyone must go outside and then you must pay to come back in again. Anycase, it gets boring afterwards because they show the same films over and over.'

'Sounds like a bargain.'

'They chip you two beers as well. Long Toms.'

'What did you see?'

'There was one about the war.'

'That's great.'

'And there was a porn show about some people in Las Vegas. On honeymoon.'

So we stroll on, side by side, shooting the breeze.

106 I have to speed on Stewart's Drive, especially at night. There's something in the powdery light on the roadway, the old rock of the ridge raked by the headlights, the arches in the stone parapet. Whether or not it was built by Italian prisoners of war (who are given credit for every decent piece of stonework in the country) this is a seaside wall, and it makes you long for water in the dip below, where the lights of Bez Valley and Kensington are flickering. My spirits lift, ascending or descending, and I put my foot down, leaning into the corners a little harder than usual.

I am in this mood one night, one early morning, as I drop down into the Valley from Yeoville. I have been drinking at Rumours and I am on my way home with a skinful of jazz. I follow the curve around the playground, accelerate to the first sharp bend and barrel through that. As the bend straightens, my lights pick out a motorcycle lying on its side in the middle of the road. The headlight is burning, pointing south. Plenty of time to brake. I ease up to the bike and go round it, looking for the rider, expecting to see him sprawled somewhere beyond the machine, but nothing. I roll down to the bottom of the hill.

I have half a mind to leave this problem for the next person and go straight home, but of course I cannot. At Terrace – Daisy de Melker's old address, it occurs to me – I turn around and go back up the hill. The fallen bike looks desolate. This time I approach more slowly. Still no sign of the rider or anyone else. Now I have no option but to go to the top of Stewart's Drive again to turn around.

As I swing into the U-turn my headlights sweep across familiar things: a tree branch poking through a wall (instead of lopping it off when he raised the wall, the builder decided to cement it into the structure) and a painted slogan – BRON YOU BISCUIT. It is impossible to turn from Stewart's Drive into Jolly Street without seeing this graffiti and wondering who and why. It has been amusing me for years, but the vanished motorcyclist has cast an uncanny light over the moment and now the dead branch reaching through the wall and the dripping message chill me. I coast back down the hill for the second time.

Another car is coming up. We both stop thirty or forty paces from the bike. We are Joburg Samaritans, wary and wily, and not particularly good. We are waiting for a sign. Finally, I get out of the car, leaving the engine running, and take a couple of steps down the hill.

Someone gets out of the other car and calls to me: 'What's going on?'

'Dunno.'

'Did you knock this guy down?'

'No ways, he saw his arse all by himself.'

We both take a few more steps towards the bike. I can smell petrol. My neck is bristling.

'Hang on a second. Don't I know you?'

'Christ! Nick. Is that you?'

'Vlad? I don't fucking believe it. What the hell are you doing here?'

'Same as you.'

I haven't seen Nicholas for years. We reach the bike at the same time and shake hands. For a moment everything seems normal, and then it seems more bizarre than ever. Like something out of *Twin Peaks*, he says, and I agree. In that spirit, we do some sleuthing: the engine of the bike is still warm, so the accident couldn't have happened too long ago. And of course the headlight is still burning. No skid marks. No sign of a collision. Key in the ignition.

'But where the fuck is this guy?'

'Perhaps he was thrown over the parapet.'

'Have you got a torch?'

'No.'

We hunt up and down along the stone wall, calling into the darkness, but get no response. We look up into the trees. We look down into the veld. In all this time, there is no sign of another vehicle, coming or going. Eventually, we have to get on with our lives, there's only so much you can do in the middle of the night. We leave the bike lying where it is, shake hands again, and go our separate ways.

At home, I call the Yeoville police station and tell them the story. It sounds like an urban legend, even to me, but they say they'll send someone.

'Be sure to take a torch.'

The bike is still there the next day and the day after, standing upright on the pavement. Then it's gone.

107 Someone turns up a video clip on a computer in the Salaries Department at police headquarters in Pretoria, showing Nelson Mandela's face morphing into that of a gorilla. President Mandela brushes the insult aside. We should not be unduly alarmed, he says, by the fact that there are racists among us. But Commissioner Jackie Selebi is furious. Although it is just eight

months since he called Sergeant Mothiba a gorilla, or rather, a chimpanzee, the Commissioner says that racism will not be tolerated in the South African Police Services. 'The employee responsible for this show of utter disrespect will face the harshest disciplinary measures permissible in terms of the regulations.'

Blenheim Street is a thoroughfare from Roberts to Kitchener, and people coming down the hill from the shops drop their peels and papers in our gutters. But when Eddie lived at No. 19, the pavement outside was always perfectly clean. He tidied up in his own way, by punting the litter downhill. The street rises steeply there, and so a cooldrink tin usually needed just one stiff kick to send it trundling off his turf. A milk carton might have to be harried all the way to the border. Eddie's law was precise: as soon as a piece of rubbish crossed into a neighbour's territory, it ceased to concern him.

Although Eddie is gone now, gravity and summer thunder-storms still ensure that most of the litter in Blenheim Street washes up on my doorstep further down the hill. There is no point in being angry with the forces of nature. From time to time, I go out with a garbage bag in one hand and a gardening glove on the other and pick everything up. In my lazy moments, I follow Eddie's example and boot a crust of bread or an orange peel or an empty mageu carton down the storm-water drain.

After a storm, everything is transformed. The cannas burst into wet flames, the dark scents of the earth seep out. Eddie's gladioli, the ones grown from the bulbs he gave me, pop magic-ally from the clean cuff of the air. The sound of water rushing in the storm-water drains makes me grateful that I am neither on top of the hill, nor down in the valley, but somewhere in between.

'Could you bring me a loaf of bread?'

109   'Sure.'

Eddie and I were chatting at his garden gate. I was going to the shop anyway and it was a small favour to ask, but he had never imposed on me before and so this signalled a new stage in our friendship. He gave me the warm coins from his pocket.

'What shall I get you then?'

'A government loaf thanks, brown, unsliced.'

The bakery at the Gem Supermarket produces round loaves and square loaves, hamburger buns and hotdog rolls, baps we identify as Italian or Portuguese, wholewheat or rye. On this day, the bins were brimming with every option except the standard brown loaf. I chose the next best thing, a wholewheat loaf with a seeded crust, and went back down the hill.

When he saw what was in the packet, Eddie's face fell. He looked so disappointed that I offered to take the loaf myself and give him his money back.

'No no, it's fine, really, one loaf is as good as the next.'

But I had failed a test. It was the last favour he ever asked of me.

'I am selling these.'

110   'No thanks.'

'Very cheap. Only ten rands.'

'I don't need one, thanks.'

'Must I be a criminal?'

'Excuse me?'

'I can be a criminal.'

'What do you mean?'

'You people, you say we mustn't do crime, so we try to sell things. Then you say we mustn't do selling.'

'I'm sorry, I didn't say you mustn't sell things, I said I'm not interested in buying what you've got. I don't need a cap, that's all.'

'Can I ask you a question?'

'Ja.'

'Will you *give* me ten rands?'

In 1966, Takis Xenopoulos opened Fontana Foods, the country's very first 24-hour bakery and takeaway, in Hillbrow's 111 High Point Centre. At the official opening, the owner made a public statement of faith in his idea: he threw the keys of the shop into the crowd. It was one of the grandest gestures ever made by a Joburger. And it seems even grander now in this barred and gated city. Somewhere, on a street free of sentry boxes and booms, we should raise a statue of Mr Xenopoulos lobbing his keys into the blue.

It has taken Chas and me the entire day to repair the carport. The new wooden crossbeams, which I bought at Tile City up 112 the road and carried down the hill over my shoulder, have been screwed into place on top of the poles. No nails for me, 60 mm screws made of brass, I mean this thing to last. By the end of the day, our palms are raw from twisting the screwdriver at awkward angles, our fingers, more used to paper and keyboard than pine and saw, are full of splinters and aching, the backs of our necks – rooinekke, that's what you can call us – are stinging from too much sun. All of these symptoms are relieved by the application of two cold Windhoek lagers, and then the carport looks like a job well done.

The next day I give the whole structure a coat of creosote, and in this acrid marinade it seems to brace itself and look sturdier than ever. I'm glad I decided against tearing it down. The shade-cloth the beams will be covered with has already been purchased at the Hypermarket in Norwood and is lying in a cool green accordion in the spare room. Next weekend I'll stretch that, and lace it tight with nylon cords, and the carport will be ready. Then all I need is a car.

The following Saturday morning, I hear a rattle at the gate. It is Ben, the builder. I see the ladder on the roof of his bakkie sticking up above the wall, and then his round face, stringy hair awry, framed in a metal diamond at the top of the gate.

I go out.

'I saw you doing this last weekend,' Ben says. 'You and Charles.' His pale eyes are round and innocent. The carport shivers.

'Yes?'

'You shouldn't have used that wood. It's going to warp.'

My heart sinks. Of course I shouldn't have used that wood, that dirt-cheap pine. That's why the bloody thing collapsed in the first place: the clot who built it used wood. Why did I have to go and copy him?

'You should have used conduit,' Ben says. The way he pronounces 'conduit', it sounds like Latin. Like some legal principle, habeas corpus, bona fides. 'Do you know what conduit is?'

'I think so.'

'This is conduit.' He pushes a piece of plastic tubing through the gap in the gate. He's been holding it in his hand, out of sight. 'It's used for electrical wiring. It's very light and strong, and it won't be damaged by sunshine or rain. It's proof against insects and creeping plants. It's also cheaper than wood. Even cheap wood. This is what you should have used.'

Conduit. I hold it in my hand like a judgement. Like the mark of a grand presumption, perhaps even a betrayal. I am still holding it after Ben has lumbered away down the hill. Conduit. It is light, strong, weather-resistant, termite-proof, cheap. It is the material I should have used instead of this third-rate pine, which is warping even as my faith in it drains away.

The old-age home at the Marymount has brought us new

152

neighbours, among them a tall man who walks with a stick.
Some malady has left him with a stiff leg, which imposes an awkward, swinging gait on him. Because of this (or so I assume) he walks in the road rather than on the pavements, occupying an entire lane with his stick and his swaying shadow, forcing cars to overtake him. Looking down on him from the stoep, I see that he has musical notes and keyholes shaved into his spiky hair like crop circles.

One morning, I happen to open the garage door just as he's passing. He stops and sways towards me, producing an item from his pocket, holding it out to me.

'I sell these to make a living, sir. Personalized key rings. Just twenty rand.'

The key ring is made of tan leather and shaped like a sow's ear. It has a silver ring through a loop on one end and is branded with a dark, smoky 'X'. For... Xavier?

'You don't have an "I" perhaps?' I ask. 'Or an "M"?'

'Let's see.' He produces a fistful of key rings from his pocket and fans them out. Five more Xs, two Zs, a Q. Surplus people.

I choose the one that's already in my hand.

Anyone can start a garden-gate telephone service: you just run an extension from the house to the front fence and set up an instrument there. You can put up a sign, if you like, advertising the rates. Later on, when you've made a bit of money, you add a metal booth, with an awning that swings up to shade the customer, and this should be painted white.

The Hillier Street cobbler has built a booth of metal sheeting and plywood. The structure is rickety and unpainted, but the swivel chair, an executive model with a high back and armrests, lends it the air of a professional office. He likes to lean back with his heels propped on a milk crate, looking like a manager.

The hawker at No. 12 Eleanor Street started with a couple of planks and tins, then added a trestle table, then a lean-to with a canvas roof. But her finest touch is a square of magic carpet laid down across the pavement. When you step from hard cement onto that soft and yielding surface, walls rise from the frayed edges of the square and for a moment you forget that you are under the sky.

People think that the informal economy rests on hard-edged things like plastic milk crates, cardboard boxes and supermarket trolleys, but it is floating on pillows of softly rounded air.

115

I came to the Johannesburg Public Library to read up on Max the Gorilla, our zoo's most famous resident, and instead I'm absorbed in a trivial mystery. Besides the usual traffic between the reference library and the reading room where I'm working, I see people coming and going through an antechamber that used to be out of bounds. In fact, the sign that says STAFF ONLY is still propped on the librarian's desk. Is there a toilet back there now? Or a new wing? It hardly seems likely when the municipal budget won't stretch to the basics like new acquisitions. What are they doing in there?

Sorry, Max. I return a bound set of the *Sunday Times* to Basil, who runs the stacks, and steel myself in the magazine corner. Then I stroll into the antechamber. It is like finding a secret passage behind a shelf of books. I half expect the voice of authority to boom, demanding the password. Stairs. I go down into grey air furred with the animal scent of old books. Scuffed Marley tiles make the place feel like a kitchen, and indeed here on a landing that ends at a closed door is a table just big enough for a kettle and a hotplate. I go down another flight and come to a barred gate through which I can see the stacks, long pent-up reaches of shelves full of books and binders. I retrace my steps to the floor above and try the door on the landing. It opens. I step out into the Harry Hofmeyr Parking Garage. This vast basement, where in years past you'd have been lucky to find a bay, is all but empty. A dozen cars are clustered around the secret entrance where I'm standing; I assume they belong to the staff and other initiates, the visitors I've seen coming and going. My own car is in a distant corner near the steps that lead up to Harrison Street. Shutting the door behind me, a featureless grey panel in a cement wall, and making a note of its location in case I ever need it again, I set out across a damp, echoey space as long as a football field.

Every new building in Johannesburg has secure, controlled, vehicle-friendly entrances and exits. The well-heeled – who naturally are also the well-wheeled – should be able to reach point B without setting foot in the street. Parking garages cling to the malls like deformed twins. Complexes of apparently independent buildings, designed to simulate the neighbourhoods of a conventional city, are undermined by huge, unitary garages that destroy the illusion. Superbasements. Older buildings have to adapt to the new requirements. The Johannesburg Art Gallery has turned its back on the public space it was designed for; instead of strolling in through Joubert Park, visitors leave their cars next to the railway line and hurry in through the back door. Elsewhere, walls have been broken through or tunnels and walkways opened up from existing basement parking garages into lobbies and reception areas. Usually these angular additions conceal their motives beneath a coat of paint, but the makeshift reversal at the Public Library is refreshingly ingenuous: while the black schoolchildren who are now the main users of the facility stroll arm-in-arm up the broad staircase from the library gardens or gather in the grand lobby to giggle and whisper, the few white suburbanites who still venture here park underground and slip in up the back stairs.

The entrance to the Joburg Metro typifies the understated charm of contemporary South African design. A corrugated afdak with a lazy slant rests on black-wattle posts, roughly dressed and creosoted, rooted in low white walls freckled with

116

mosaic. The Metro-Net logo is picked out in ox-blood and mercury on the lintel. You enter the cage and it drops into the gloom. Light your lamp. You pass through lava and sediment into prehistory, falling back in time towards the pyritic ores of the Main Reef. At last, in the neighbourhood of hell, as you imagine it, the cage shudders to a halt and the doors open. Mind the gap. But you cannot step out at all because the opening is blocked by a sheet of rock. You lean towards this rich confection, a blue conglomerate studded with almond-quartz, and press your tongue to it. The smoky pebbles taste of salt. Swallowing sand, you remember the sign in the window of the ticket booth. Take your pick.

'I don't want to live under this thing.'

117   We are curving from the M2 East onto Harrow Road and by the tilt of his head Branko means the new Coca-Cola sign on top of Ponte. His declaration of independence is too earnest for my liking. I say:

'Have you forgotten the one on the Durban beachfront? Things go better with Coke.' We saw this sign on a family holiday in the sixties, an immense reservoir of effervescent light bulbs with a neon straw three storeys long sticking out of it, drained and replenished and drained a thousand times a day, a perpetual slaking of an insatiable thirst.

'That was different.'

'You couldn't get enough of the spectacle. The old man had to drive past it fifty times, until the rest of us felt sick. All those lights fizzing up in red and black waves.'

'That had style,' he protests again, bending until his chin touches the dash to look up at Ponte's fifty storeys, elongating as we draw closer. 'This thing is vulgar. And the size of it! Do you know it consumes as much juice as the whole building? That scrap of neon in Durbs would look like a postage stamp beside this monster. It's like they've stuck a label on the whole city, as if it belonged to them.'

'The reason you hate it so much is that it's damaged the sky-line. You can't cope with the slightest change. I thought I was bad, but you're three times worse.'

'Three? You know, they wanted to sign their name on the moon. Didn't you tell me that?'

This was a couple of years ago. Today Branko calls me in a mood. 'Have you seen what they've done to Ponte? They've replaced the Coke sign with a hideous thing for Vodacom, blue and green hoops flickering up and down on the tip of the tower. You'd think it was an advert for condoms.'

When my brother and my sister and I were growing up in Pretoria, Johannesburg was further away than it is now. The 118 people there spoke English, the buildings were taller, the streets were dirty and dangerous, the drivers – the TJ drivers, we called them derisively, after their number plates – were fast and reck-less. Real cowboys. It was almost another country, a suspicion confirmed by the adoption of the decimal system, which widened the distance between the two cities from a familiar thirty-five miles to a foreign sixty kilometres. Halfway House, a clutch of shops and houses that lay midway, had come by its name, as my dad never tired of telling us, in the days when the trip used to take so long travellers had to outspan overnight. Even in the sixties, the road through the veld was narrow and crooked, bluegums and pines dawdled beside it, and it was easy to imagine ox-wagons and tin lizzies passing through the shadows. Coming or going, the wagons would have belonged in our city and the motor cars in theirs. Despite the Zephyrs and Zodiacs, Volkswagen Beetles and Hillman Imps that progress had bestowed on Pretoria, we felt like people who had been left behind, who were not fast enough.

Apart from annual pilgrimages to see the Rand Easter Show and the Christmas lights in Joubert Park, we went to Joburg only for special occasions like family weddings or soccer matches. After a game at Balfour Park my dad would buy supper for Branko and me at Panburgers, a takeaway place off a service road on Louis Botha Avenue. The service road itself was a sign of the city's American dream-life. In fact, the whole length of Louis Botha, named though it was after the Afrikaner Prime Minister and Boer War general, was an American way, jammed with American cars and lined with American businesses.

Panburgers was a clash of red and white stripes, sizzling grills and chiming cash registers. Heaps of pale chips lay glistening in glass tanks like aquariums. The cooldrinks were mostly crushed ice, the straws were made of plastic, the cooks wrapped the burgers in waxed paper and called them 'panburgers', as if they had invented a marvellous new foodstuff. The kitchen staff were the usual black men, but the counter hands were white children, the unnaturally pale progeny of Bramley Gardens and Savoy Estate. Pretoria children were hard and brown from the sun and bristly; Joburg children had floppy fringes and soft freckled hands and looked as if they never went outside. Yet all the fun we had riding bicycles and kicking soccer balls counted for nothing because they were in here working, wearing paper hats and striped aprons as if they were in an Archie comic. They were already kids and we were still children.

119 As he's running along the Braamfontein Spruit early one morning, Mike sees a man lounging on a scrap of wasteland beneath a pylon, right beside the footpath. Mike is visiting the country, he's heard the stories about people getting mugged for nothing more than their shoes, and so he's wary. He slows down, considers turning back. But now he's close enough to recognize the man: it's the gardener of the townhouse complex where he's staying, apparently relaxing before he reports for duty, smoking the first cigarette of the day. The man recognizes him at the same moment and calls a greeting. Mike stops to chat. Their

paths have crossed half a dozen times in the past week around the complex, and Mike was struck by his surly submissiveness, but now he seems forthright and approachable. Meeting here on no-man's-land has freed him to be a different person. Or rather, has freed them to stand in a different relation to one another, because Mike realizes that he must also be a different person, here. When the gardener lights his second cigarette, Mike takes one too, although he's trying to cut down, although he's in the middle of a run. They talk for twenty minutes about work and soccer and politics, and then it's time to go back into the past, where their old selves are waiting.

The J&C Café in Harrow Road has two plate-glass windows painted over with signs, the one advertising the necessities – 120 fresh bread (daily!), pies, chicken pieces, cigarettes, magazines – the other, Coca-Cola. Suddenly it comes back to me: I saw that sign being painted. Might have been when I was living in Mount Verna in Saunders Street. I had been reading Woody Guthrie's *Bound for Glory*, and signwriting struck me as a very fine trade. Woody Guthrie was a true artist, equally at ease painting a sign on a barn or a copy of Whistler's *Mother*. Once, when a cop asked him what kind of work he did, he said, 'Painter. Signs. Pictures. Houses. Anything needs paintin'.' And this signwriter at the J&C, a coloured guy in a blue overall, with chunky black hair like a Hollywood Inca, he had flair too (although I doubt he had sables from Russia, the best that money can buy). Having chalked the whole design onto a red ground, he was now applying the paint. He was working on the initial C, filling in the flourish that breaks like a wave under Coca-, using a maulstick with a rubber pad as plump as a marshmallow. Making things difficult for himself. Surely it would be easier to do the letters from left to right and put the flourish in afterwards? Perhaps the initial had a momentum he could not resist and he needed to finish it in one gesture, curving the white surf to its breaking, always-about-to-break edge.

Here I am, twenty years later, gazing at his handiwork from my car as I wait for the lights to change, poetry tingling on my tongue like sherbet. All at once I begin to doubt my memory. I can see the signwriter as clear as day, but the place is vague. How can I be sure it was this sign, of all signs, when its reasonable facsimiles are scattered all over the city? Twenty years is a long time. I shift the signwriter around in my mind, superimposing him and his maulstick, and a short wooden ladder that has appeared unbidden in the frame, against the front of the café in Saunders Street opposite the Happy Autumn Home. He fits there. I put him against the Norana Bakery and Supermarket in Bellevue East. Fits there too. I try the Kenmere side of the Apollo Café in Yeoville, opposite the municipal baths – that window was broken for half a year, I recall, they must have replaced it. When was that? There. I move him from one corner café to another, wandering further and further from home, and even as the places become less familiar (Maha-Vij's Provisions in Derby Road, Bertrams, the Medusa Street window of the Rhodes Park Supermarket and Takeaways, the Jules Street side of the Marathon Café in Malvern), the signwriter grows more vivid.

For years, we knew the double-storey at the bottom of Albemarle Street as the Gandhi House. In the decade before the Great War, we'd been told, Gandhi lived here with his family. Now the house has lost its claim on history (but not its plaque from the National Monuments Council). An enterprising researcher, with nothing to gain by this unmasking except the truth, has shown that Gandhi did not live here after all, but up the road at No. 11. One of Gandhi's descendants, who visited the house as a child, has provided confirmation. The people at No. 11 should have that plaque moved to their wall.

Both the Gandhi Houses, the true and the false, are double-

121

storeys set on a promontory between two thoroughfares, but the attitudes of the streets could not differ more. Hillier and Albemarle Streets approach the impostor rather kindly, cupping it in leafy palms, whereas Albemarle and Johannes grip the genuine article like an egg in a nutcracker.

No. 11 has a handsome corrugated-iron roof and a wide, shady balcony. I recall an ornate wrought-iron finial, the ECG of a Victorian heartbeat, dancing along the roof ridge, but it must have been removed by the renovators. I cannot remember ever seeing a person on the balcony, perfectly suited though it is to reading the paper or chatting over sundowners, but for a few years there were shop-window mannequins leaning on the parapet. Perhaps they were scarecrows for thieves? At night, with the lighted windows behind them, they always deceived the eye. Something in the atmosphere, a bit of lace around the neck, a reddish tinge to the light from the doorway, made them look like whores.

Apparently, the Mahatma used to take his rest on the balcony on summer nights. It is easy to picture him there with sleep in his eyes, buffing his little round glasses on the hem of a bed sheet.

The war memorial crumbling away on a traffic island opposite the Darras Centre tells the history of the city in a single word. 'The following men of the Bezuidenhout Valley lost their lives in the Great War,' it says, and then follows a list of names, some of them scarred by graffiti, others drifting away into the depths of the stone where the leafy reflection of an overhanging oak stirs. A century comes and goes in the definite article. When this memorial was commissioned, the Bezuidenhout Valley was still a feature of the landscape. Now it is impossible to think of 'Bezuidenhout Valley' as anything but a suburb.

Impossible. I have walked along this pavement a thousand times,

122

there isn't a detail I could have missed, never mind something so big. And such a peculiar, pointless thing too.

I go back, fearfully. It's still there. A metal pole slightly taller than me, the bottom third painted black, the rest silver. It is too thick for its height: something so sturdily rooted should be as tall as a street light, whereas I could touch the top of it with the point of a new pencil. I try to throttle it, but my fingers barely reach halfway round. It appears to be solid: when I kick against it with the toe of my boot, I get nothing but a dull thud, as if it's packed with cork. On top is a turnip-shaped stopper, apparently welded to the shaft. Has it been lopped and plugged? Or was it made like this? If it isn't a telephone pole or a street light cut down to size... then what is it? Exactly?

Context. Stone wall behind belongs to No. 17 Roberts Avenue, well built, expertly mortared. Sign on the letterbox beside the gate says INDEPENDENT PATHOLOGY SERVICES. Second box with a wider slot to receive specimens for the attention of various doctors. Through the bars of the gate, a yard with space for two or three cars (only one there now).

I cannot believe that the doctors have anything to do with this. It's like something out of *2001: A Space Odyssey*. I can imagine that it was put here by an alien or left behind by an ancient civilization whose monuments I am incapable of recognizing.

The next day, I take Minky up the road and make the introductions.

'Have you seen this thing before?' I ask.

'I don't think so. What is it?'

'You tell me.'

'Looks like a pole. A short pole.'

'Yes.'

'What's it for?'

'Beats me.'

She looks at it from another angle. 'I like it. Must be the same Victorian vintage as the Yeoville water tower. It's like a little minaret in Omar Khayyam.'

'Yes. But what's it *for*?'

I have been passing this thing for years without seeing it, but now that it's made itself visible it insists on being acknowledged every time. I look out for it, imagining it from a block away. No sooner have I turned the corner from Blenheim into Roberts than I anticipate its compellingly useless presence. I hope it will have vanished and dread that possibility too. It has become an anchor. No, it is more firmly rooted in the earth than that, it is a bollard to which an anchor might be secured.

Saturdays are quieter than Sundays on Roberts Avenue. On the Sabbath, you are likely to meet lost tribes of Zionists in salt-white robes, bearing wooden drums and long staffs that wriggle like snakes; or teams of soccer players jogging to the pitch, keeping time with the drum-bounce of a ball. On a Saturday afternoon, then, I stroll up to Roberts Avenue with a tape measure in my pocket. Height: 2.5 metres. Circumference: 70 centimetres. There are no other dimensions. It resists reduction. So I carry these facts home, height and circumference, two dense figures, compact as seeds.

A year later one of the seeds germinates. What grows is a tomason.

The term 'tomason' was coined by Genpei Akasegawa to describe a purposeless object found on a city street. He has tracked and tagged hundreds of them in Japan and other parts of the world. A tomason is a thing that has become detached from its original purpose. Sometimes this detachment may be so complete that the object is turned into an enigmatic puzzle; alternatively, the original purpose of the object may be quite apparent and its current uselessness touching or amusing. It may be a remnant of a larger fixture that has been taken away, or it may be a thing complete in itself, whose purpose has been forgotten. Perhaps the people who put it there, who used it and needed it, have moved away or died. Perhaps the trade it was meant to serve is no longer practised. The natural habitat of the tomason is the city street. This is not to say that tomasons cannot be found in the countryside, but they are so scarce there that hunting for them would be tedious. Tomasons thrive in the man-made world, in spaces that are constantly being remade and redesigned for other purposes, where the function of a thing that was useful and necessary may be swept away in a tide of change or washed off like a label. They are creatures of the boundary, they gravitate to walls and fences, to entrances and exits. You will find them attached to facades or jutting out of pavements, like the short pole in Roberts Avenue.

I am grateful to have been given a category that will hold certain chance observations so tidily. More than that, it is a category that casts the world in a different light: having discovered a new shade of interest, I now seem to notice it everywhere. The tilt of my head has been altered and significance flares up in odd places. Every day I trawl along my habitual routes ready to be startled by something else I have missed until now. After a while, however, this deliberate hunt begins to foul the workings of chance, which is one of the pleasures of walking. My focus narrows. Details snag me, every bracket or niche has become a puzzle. Is this a true tomason? Or a doubting tomason whose apparently mysterious function will suddenly become clear? The world at large is lost to me. As my eye becomes attuned to everything that is extraneous, inconspicuous and minor, that is abandoned or derelict, the obvious, useful facts of the city recede and a hidden history of obsolescence comes to the surface. Every time I go walking, I stumble right out of the present. In the end, it is a relief when I have gleaned what I can from the edges of my neighbourhood and the conscious enterprise fades to the back of my mind.

When Henion finished cutting his film *A letter to my cousin in China*, he invited us to a viewing. We walked down to his house in Cambrian Street on a summer evening after supper. On the pavement outside, a security guard was sitting on a white plastic chair with his fingers laced behind his head, chatting to a

124

domestic worker from the neighbourhood. We buzzed and Henion let us in. The kids had been swimming: a trail of wet footprints led from the pool to the verandah steps. Henion showed us into his studio, a room of cool, calm surfaces and lightly accented space, where African and Chinese objects conversed in low tones.

That was three years ago. Last night, Minky and I watched the documentary again on video. A lot has happened to us in the interim – we've been abroad and come back again, Henion and Lee have left for Australia – and this overshadowed my understanding of the film. Then I thought it revolved around the ideas of mortality and home. Now I see that I should have paid more attention to a suckling baby, a grieving widow clutching a dead man's jacket, a group portrait. It is about physical intimacy with the feeling body and its unfeeling remains.

In a memorable scene, Henion's father, Chi Ho Han, practises acupuncture upon himself to still the pain of his terminal cancer. Is he struggling to find the exact spot because of failing powers? No, the struggle is rather a sign of precision. As he probes beneath his skin with the point of the needle, a hidden network of nerve comes to the surface, like an acupuncturist's chart concealed in his own flesh. This sense of intimacy with flesh and blood is heightened because he behaves as if he is alone, although he is not, the narrating camera is also there, yet so close, so much a part of himself as to have made itself invisible. Probing with the needle, he reveals an aged body, a ragged toenail, the relief of veins, as nakedly as any lover in his prime.

In the following scene, the old man appears to be drifting in and out of sleep. His glasses cast a film of light over his eyes. Earlier we have seen him asleep; later we will see him in his coffin. On this last occasion, the camera goes to his eyes, beneath the glasses – yes, the corpse is wearing glasses – to touch the jagged line of a sealed lid. Has the eye been sewn shut? Of these three views – the sleeping man, breathing yet oblivious; the man on the verge of sleep, fading in and out of consciousness; the dead man, blind and unfeeling – it is the middle man who stays with me.

Chi Ho Han is dead now and buried in Los Angeles, as far from Wenchang where he was born as from Johannesburg where he spent most of his life. His wife and mother, or rather their substances gathered into twinned ossuaries, are buried beside him. For his father, Henion says, the important thing was proximity. You had to be close together. You had to feel the shoulder of the person beside you against your own. That gentle pressure on the body is the sense of belonging.

125   Minky and I talk about moving, but we're afraid of what might happen to the pagoda tree in our garden.

When Glynis sold her house in Johannes Street, the new owner chopped down the trees. The first time she went back, she had to step over the trunk of a palm she had nursed to adulthood, swathing it in hessian every winter against the frost until it was tall enough to fend for itself. She cannot bring herself to go there again. She sends Sean to collect the mail.

In those Joburg suburbs where the stands are small nearly every front garden has made way for a carport or a parking bay. Often the space in front of a semi is so cramped you wouldn't think a car could fit there. For a while, one of my neighbours had a parking problem: the bay carved out of his front yard wasn't quite long enough for his bakkie and he had to park it on the diagonal, with the two gates angled outwards and joined by a chain. When he acquired a second vehicle, a better solution had to be found. So he employed a burglar-proofer to weld an extension onto the existing gate, a cage half a metre deep that allows the tail ends of both vehicles to stick out over the pavement.

Periodically, the municipality savages the oaks on Kitchener Avenue, cuts them down to size to remind them that they're in Africa. They line the streets, showing us their stumps, and we feel sorry for them, although there is nothing we can do. In spring, they grow a fuzz of leaves, and become big-headed and tender. Then every stump shoots out a clutch of long straight water shoots. They are never themselves again. With their new limbs standing on end, they look permanently startled, deranged. The aloes in between lean out towards the street like old people waiting for a funeral procession.

Dave comes home from the bush with a dozen saplings on the back of his bakkie. There are no exotics among them, our city is full of those, the newcomers are all locals. And they are not for his own garden, which has already spilled over onto the pavement, they are for us. He plants them a block away, on the verge in Barossa Street opposite the Wits Mental Health Society. The young trees wear their names on paper bracelets around their skinny wrists, where I could discover them if I chose, or I could ask Dave to call the roll by heart, but the rhythm of walking without stepping on the cracks makes me invent: naboom, boerboon, melkhout, ash, yellowwood, ironwood, umbrella tree.

Details (Route 1)

126

4 Kitchener

This house once had a beautiful fence of wrought-iron vines and sawtooth leaves. In the summer, nasturtiums would twine up and fleck their pale stems among the green-painted iron ones. Then a scrap-metal scavenger snapped off all the iron leaves, clean as figs, and left the jagged stems pointing to holes in the air.

38 Kitchener

A house in two minds. Having stripped it of every curve and kink, squared it off and cemented it over, the builder decided that it needed a softer touch after all and put three rounded

167

arches in the facade; and then, doubting himself again, sank a square window frame in one of them. The high wall is topped with curly wrought-iron panels salvaged from the low wall it superseded, but they look strangely displaced at that height, with the sky behind them rather than the garden. The pillars end in cement globes like cannonballs. On the roof of the stoep a plaster eagle, an ugly bird bought from a nursery as an embellishing touch. Could the same person who hacked the features off this house possibly have tethered that bird of prey up there? It was meant to evoke ruined grandeur, but instead it reeks of the graveyard; it belongs in the Church of the Holy Angels across the way.

83 Kitchener
On the whitewashed gable, like a holiday destination on the front of a bus: THE KLOOFS.

94 Kitchener
The garden path leads to an impregnable barrier of spiky palisades; only the postbox is there to mark the spot where the gate in the old fence must have been.

105 Kitchener
White plastered walls with the texture of coconut ice, split into crazy paving by forked black lines. It looks as if someone dropped the house and broke it into a hundred pieces.

110 Kitchener
Three cement frogs, each squatting in its own plastic pot, ranged along the garden path like plants.

118 Kitchener
Dr Z. Ebrahim's Surgery has a black palisade fence. A solitary, truncated palisade, just thirty centimetres high including its elaborately spiked crown, is bolted to the top of a pillar in the corner of the garden. It stands on this pedestal like an African

idol in the Musée de l'Homme.

141 Kitchener

The tiler who lives here has turned his yard into a chaotic catalogue of ornamental stone. It is paved with offcuts of every variety, and more are stacked against the wall of the house, ready to
be applied to other surfaces. The only order in the patchwork is
created by three cement pots like goldfish bowls set into the
paving at regular intervals and holding nothing but dark-brown
earth. Beside the front door is a fourth pot with cacti jutting
from it like spiky truncheons.

3 Broadway

Wavy pillars studded with mud-brown stones on the stoep and
patches of tan slate on the gable. Together these features invari-
ably make me think of giraffes.

City centre (Route 2)

Go east on Jules Street – he says – all the way to the end.   127
Just before the kink, take a right into Stanhope. You'll see the
Pure & Cool roadhouse on your left (hope it's still there). Keep
on for a kilometre or two, past the rubbish dump and the
vehicle testing grounds. At the second or third set of lights
there's a Caltex on the left and one of those outdoor workshops opposite, with exhaust pipes propped up in tripods or
strung on lines like wind chimes. Turn right and go down
towards the railway line. Just after the crossing take the fork to
the left and you're nearly there. This is mining land. Bluegums
on one side, open veld on the other. Look out for the sign that
points to the shooting range. Just after that there's a dirt road
where you can make a U-turn. Drive back towards the city for
a bit and you'll see a lay-by. Park there.

Go at the end of winter. If you're lucky, a fire will have
turned the khaki cotton of the veld to black velvet. Loose

threads of smoke are still drifting up, the air smells burnt at the edges.

Engage the Gorilla and get out of the car.

The veld slopes down to a highway in the south. On the far side, the sawtooth roofs of factories, the rutted flanks of a mine dump. These are the leavings of the mine whose head-gear you can see on the horizon in the west, like a model made of matchsticks, an engine of war. The sky is the colour of a week-old bruise. You may hear the whisper of traffic on Main Reef Road, the crack of rifle shots at the range, which is carved out of another dump among the gums. In the east, beyond that billboard advertising Caesar's, you will find a vlei full of poisoned water and a suburb cowering beneath power lines.

Now you must go into the veld – don't forget your walking shoes – slowly, there's no rush. Crystals of black ash and charred stalks as brittle as the wing bones of birds shatter under your soles. Already assegais of new grass are thrusting through the scorched earth, prickling your eyes with their pointed green. The black crust crackles underfoot like remembered flames. 'Charcoal on the hoof.' What are you looking for? – a greasy bottle with a Smirnoff label. half a brick with a scab of cement and an iron rod twisting out of it. a flattened tin. the foundations of a ruined substation. three porcelain insulators thrown down from the pylons by the Escom electricians, as beautifully wrought as vases. a burnt-out bulb. a signature. smudged lines. pencil stubs.

Are you still with me? In this dog-eared field, collapsing from one attitude to another, dragging your ghosts through the dirty air, your train of cast-off selves, constantly discovering yourself at the centre, in the present.

19 Barossa
'Please open or nock hard' (black marker on white sheet metal)

cnr Benbow & Barossa
'Wits Mental Health Society' (red and black enamel on white sheet metal)

Pavement, Benbow
'Stan the Happy Man' (blue aerosol on cement paving)

cnr Kitchener & Benbow
'black'? 'blank'? (black aerosol tag on steel Marymount Nursing Home sign)

21/21a Kitchener
'Tuck Shop and Salon' professionally prepared spaza sign. numbers on wall partly obscured by new municipal power box (enamel on board)

Vallivue Centre, cnr Kitchener & Appolonia (north-facing wall)
'Salon Africa. We do braiding and relax. 083 9600 052' (enamel on board)

Embankment, East Side College
'If you DON'T speak out about HIV/AIDS, it becomes a burden – John, HIV Positive' message clear, but name of author fading away (white and blue enamel on cement)

Embankment, East Side College
'Nelson's Panelbeating, Sppaypanting and repairs to Bumpers and Dash Broads' (spray-paint on cement)

Vallivue Centre, cnr Kitchener & Appolonia (rooftop)
'The Gravity Addict' (unknown)

cnr Appolonia & Nourse
'Phone & what-what. Bar & pool' double 'o' in 'pool' pictured as 3 ball (green) and 12 ball (blue) (PVA on painted plaster)

Gem Pawn Brokers, Albemarle
'Time will tell, Christ or Hell!' (black aerosol on yellow PVA)

Gem Pawn Brokers, Roberts
'These premises has been wired with razorwire!' final word rests on spiky underlining of electrified barbs (gloss enamel on hardboard)

6 Roberts
'JiC' geometric monogram (black aerosol on white PVA)

Gem Supermarket, Blenheim
'Salvation!' (black aerosol on advertising chalkboard headed 'Today's Special')

Substation, Blenheim
jailbird with stubble, shaven head (black aerosol on beige PVA)

Substation, Blenheim
'blank'? 'black'? (black aerosol tag on beige PVA)

129   'Now I don't mean to be insulting like,' says Ben, 'but your plumber is useless.' And he waits for me to say:
      'How so?'
      'These taps are the wrong way round.' And he waits again for:
      'Why?'
      'The hot tap in the bath should always be against the wall.'
      'Why?'
      'If a toddler comes in here, see, and wants to open one of

these taps, chances are he'll try the one that's closest to him. And if it's the cold, then he won't scald himself. Maybe he won't even be able to reach the hot if it's at the back. Plumbers are supposed to know these things.'

The oaks in Roberts Avenue have shackles around their ankles. **130** These iron hoops, which were used to edge the holes when the saplings were planted, look like the rims of wagon-wheels. With the thickening of their trunks and spreading of their roots, the growing trees have often dislodged the hoops from the paving, breaking them loose into the air. Sometimes bark has grown over part of the hoop, sealing it, healing it into the woody flesh. I imagine that here and there a tree must have engulfed its shackle entirely. My friend Liz says the shackles are there to stop the trees from wandering off, the poor things are no better than slaves. My brother Branko says she's read too much Tolkien, it's the other way round: the trees are there to keep the shackles from being stolen.

Johannesburg is a frontier city, a place of contested boundaries. **131** Territory must be secured and defended or it will be lost. Today the contest is fierce and so the defences multiply. Walls replace fences, high walls replace low ones, even the highest walls acquire electrified wires and spikes. In the wealthier suburbs the pattern is to knock things flat and start all over. Around here people must make the most of what they've already got, and therefore the walls tend to grow by increments. A stone wall is heightened with prefab panels, a prefab wall is heightened with steel palisades, the palisades are topped with razor wire. Wooden pickets on top of brick, ornate wrought-iron panels on top of plaster, blade wire on top of split poles. These piggyback walls (my own included) are nearly always ugly. But sometimes the whole ensemble achieves a degree of elaboration that becomes beautiful again, like a page in the *Homemaker's Fair* catalogue.

The tomason of access is our speciality. There are vanished gateways everywhere. On any street, you may find a panel in a wall where the bricks are a different colour or the courses poorly aligned, indicating that a gap has been filled in. A garden path leads to a fence rather than a gate, a doorstep juts from the foot of a solid wall. Often, the addition of a security fence or a wall has put a letterbox beyond reach of the postman. The ghosts come and go.

The tennis courts at the corner of Collingwood and Roberts are on a terrace. Once, a flight of stairs cut into the stone-faced slope led up from the pavement, and then a few paces would bring you to a gate in a low wire fence. Now a curtain of stone has been drawn across the stairway halfway up and a tall palisade fence raised on the edge of the terrace, through which you can see the old fence posts, like sentries standing guard on a fallen frontier.

The most common tomason of access by far is the metal hinge. Set into brick or stone gate posts, and thus too difficult or costly to remove, these hinges remain behind to mark the places where the old gates swung, before they were taken down and replaced by security doors or remote-controlled barriers.

132   When I lived in Eleanor Street, I used to pass by No. 13 on my way to the shops. One day I saw a man pottering in the garden and we nodded to one another, and from time to time after that we exchanged a greeting or a wave. Then I moved to Malvern. After David Webster was killed outside his house, Chas, who had been a student of his at Wits, took me past there to pay his respects. And it was only then that I put the man in the news reports together with my nodding acquaintance from the old neighbourhood.

Whether it's because I only ever saw him in his garden, or

read somewhere that he'd just come back from the nursery and was unloading plants from his bakkie when he was shot, I often wonder whether he planted the creepers and shrubs still thriving in the yard. Gardeners must have faith in the future. What became of the seedlings he bought that morning? Did his widow get round to planting them? Did someone remember to water them? Or were they left to wither in their black plastic bags?

The mosaic that commemorates his life spills along the garden wall. The panel on the left says: 'DAVID WEBSTER 1940-1989. Assassinated here in the name of apartheid. Lived for peace, justice and friendship.' The rest of it is a surf of brightly coloured tiles and glittering mirrors that turns the wall to water.

Wherever I go in Joburg, I bump into Herman Charles Bosman. 133 I see him at the City Hall, talking from the steps or heckling from the edge of a crowd; gazing into a shop window in Eloff Street, barefooted and in his shirtsleeves, suffering from the recognizing blues; marching at the end of a procession along Commissioner Street; enquiring after books at the desk in the Public Library (where he is supposed to have met his second wife, Ella Manson); strolling along under the oaks at Jeppe Boys' High on his way home to Grace Street. Long past midnight, he is wandering down Plein Street with his friend George, so deep in conversation they don't even see me. And there he is again scrambling up the side of a mine dump with Ella (they are going to write their poems in the sand). And climbing over the wall of the municipal tram sheds.

Most vividly of all, I see him at High Court Buildings in Joubert Street where he had an office in the forties, standing on a tiny second-floor balcony – it is no more than a crow's-nest with a flagpole sticking out of it like a sail yard – scattering seed for the pigeons. This is curious, because Bosman himself never described the scene in his work. Rather, it was Lionel Abrahams who saw him there, 'shirt-sleeved, bare-headed, sunlit, in a cloud of fluttering birds', and brought the moment to life in his memoir 'Mr Bosman'. It is the privilege of writers that they are able to invent their memories and pass them on between the covers of a book, to make their memories ours.

Speaking of Abrahams, I bump into him too all over town, although these days he can seldom be lured from his house in Rivonia. I see him further along Joubert Street on his way to Vanguard Books (he is going in search of a copy of Rosamond Lehmann's *The Weather in the Streets*). I bump into him on top of a mine dump too – he has gone up there with some friends to read Herbert and Holub. One of my dearest memories has him waiting for the tram at the stop outside his house in Roberts Avenue. Again – let's not consider it odd – this is not my memory but someone else's, passed on in a book.

Lionel Abrahams has written about the significance that certain stray corners of the city assume through personal association, places where we feel more alive and more at home because a 'topsoil of memory' has been allowed to form there. Louise Masreliez is concerned with the 'private niches' memory creates in the public space of the city. The image aptly suggests the small and fugitive nature of the association (a 'niche' may be as fleeting as a mood or atmosphere). Both writers present memory in intriguingly concrete terms. Whether as topsoil or niche, whether substance or receptacle, memory is endowed with a hand-warmingly physical quality. This most intimate faculty, residing in the heart or the mind, in the softest organs, might yet carve out or fill a space in the material world. So we allow parts of ourselves to take root and assume a separate life. These marks, the places where our thoughts and feelings have brushed against the world, are not just for ourselves. We are like tramps, leaving secret signs for those who come after us, whom we expect to speak the same language. Our faith in the music of this double address, in the echo chambers of the head and the street, helps to explain why apartheid deafened us to the call of home.

Every year, Piet Retief goes away for Christmas, not to Durban,   134
I've decided, which is the mythical holiday destination of
tramps, but to some farm in the Free State, where the child in
him is remembered and loved. The people at home, *die mense by*
die huis, parents, brothers and sisters, ex-lovers and old school-
friends, believe his lies about the city, or pretend to. I want him
to have a happy story.

The weather's thumb crushes stone to gravel and rubs wood   135
down to the grain. What comes to the surface is stubborn. Our
meanings are tender sheaths, but the heart of things is fibre and
flint, and will not yield to the hand or the eye.

A hand slipped here. This pane is spattered with paint from
the bristles of a brush. The glass whispers its secrets to my
fingertips, tells them the colour of a wall that cannot be seen.
But here a hand meant to leave a mark. On this pane, in a
moment of anger, idleness or thoughtless delight, fingers
toothed with a coin or a key scratched out the view.

Where am I? Another window stops me in my tracks. But
the eye goes on ahead, it plunges through glass, between bars,
through cracks into the other room. The other room is almost
there, a trick of light and shadow. The eye explores its sudden
edges and returns with a warning: the wide world is at your
back.

Yang-Ti, the second and last emperor of the Sui dynasty,   136
ascended the throne in 604 after assassinating his father. He was
one of the great builders in Chinese history, commissioning
palaces and extending the Great Wall, and sparing no cost in
materials, labour and the lives of workers. He built the city of
Lo-Yang, the second of his capitals, on the edge of the eastern
plains, and the Grand Canal, which linked the city with the

southern capital of Chiang-tu on the Yangtze river. Like his father, the emperor was a generous patron of art and literature, and painting flowered during his short reign. The frescoes of the Sui dynasty were matchless.

When Yang-Ti went travelling to the outposts of his empire, he took with him a painting on silk two thousand paces long. Every evening when a halt was called, his painters and soldiers unwound the silk and spanned it in an immense circle, like a laager, and the emperor rested within. The painting, as complete as the horizon, showed a prospect of Lo-Yang. To the south, over the roofs and battlements and the suburbs where the tradesmen lived, the mountains. To the west, the setting sun. To the north, the black lands where the ancestors were buried, the furrowed hills full of sepulchres. To the east, where the moon was swimming, the forecourts of palaces, ministries, halls of justice, houses of pleasure. In the middle of his resting tent, in a small tower, the emperor dwelt, suspended in space and time, between west and east, yesterday and tomorrow. Even in the desert, Yang-Ti kept his city with him, believing that it was unbecoming for an emperor to live like a vagabond in the wilderness. He would not countenance a change of scenery.

Victor Segalen: 'That was not understood in his time. Yang-Ti left behind the reputation of an egoist and a sedentary, since, true to Himself, he disliked to contemplate the world in any other way but at its centre.'

137   The Argonaut Mine was first proposed in the early nineties. It has been estimated that this ultra-deep mine, operating at up to five kilometres below the surface, would cost R8 billion to commission. The developer, Durban Roodepoort Deep, is conducting a feasibility study and the decision on whether to proceed will be made in 2007. Argonaut would undermine a huge swathe of the Witwatersrand, stretching from Roodepoort in the west to Boksburg in the east, in an arc roughly thirty kilometres

long and ten kilometres wide. Examine any map of this land and the goldfields ghost through from below. The names of the companies that pegged the original claims are honeycombed into the ground beneath our feet: Durban Roodepoort Deep, Vogelstruisfontein, Consolidated Main Reef, Crown Mines, Robinson Deep, City Deep, Simmer and Jack. The developer of Argonaut has some revolutionary ideas for the mine, such as generating electricity on site using subterranean water flows, partially processing the ore before it is conveyed to the surface, and housing the miners themselves in underground hostels.

As I'm coasting down the ramp to the Harry Hofmeyr Parking Garage, I remember the back way into the reading room, which I discovered the last time I came to the library. Should I use that door? I'm not sure I'll be able to find it. Anyway, I should resist this scurrying about underground, this mole-like secretiveness. I park as usual near the cashiers' booth, take the tiled tunnel under Harrison Street and go up the steps that come out beside the City Hall. I like the walk, never mind the broken paving stones and hawkers' clutter. I want to approach the library along a city street like an ordinary citizen, passing from the company of people into the company of books. I won't go sneaking up the back stairs like a thief.

I cross over Harrison and pass the cenotaph. The library gardens are full of people. It looks like a rally of sorts. Men, men in uniform, thousands of them, a ragtag army in blue, black and grey fatigues, wearing berets of every colour, combat boots, flashes on their sleeves.

'What's happening?' I ask the man next to me at the Simmonds Street crossing.

'Strike,' he says. 'Security guards' strike.'

Cut-off whitey, he's thinking to himself, doesn't know what's going on. Actually, I've read about the strike, and I know the library gardens have long been a rallying point for popular causes, but I wasn't aware the strikers were gathering here. Probably wouldn't have made the trip if I'd known. There's a current of tension in the air and it swirls round me as I approach the hawkers' stalls, a mood as pungent as the smoke from the braziers where women are roasting mielies and frying thick coils of wors in a froth of yellow fat. Up ahead, on the plaza in front of the library, between the lawns and the stairs ascending grandly to the main doors, a man is speaking through a megaphone. Perhaps the tension is rippling out from him? He could be announcing a breakthrough or a deadlock in the negotiations. Who are they negotiating with? One can guess at the issues: wages, benefits, conditions of employment. I climb up on a bench so that I can see the man with the megaphone over the heads of the crowd. There's a statue to the left of the plaza, a family group in bronze, and he's joined them on the pedestal, hooking a comradely arm through one of theirs. A knot of men at the pond on the right. What are they doing? Some sort of tussle going on in the water, it looks like a baptism or a drowning. All these berets. You can tell by their headgear which of the companies are run by military men, the out-of-work soldiers of the old SADF: these guards wear their berets moulded tightly to their heads, scraped down over their right ears, whereas the guards employed by businessmen have soft, spongy berets, mushrooms and marshmallows no real soldier would be seen dead in.

Familiar faces on all sides. There are security guards everywhere in Joburg, and now they all look like people I've seen before. If I had time I could probably spot Bongi, the apprentice security guard from my faraway birthday party. He must be a seasoned pro by now and uniformed from boot to beret. Strangers keep catching my eye, casing my white features. No doubt they're wondering what the hell I'm doing here. This thought could make me apprehensive, except that no one focuses on me for long, their attention keeps being tugged to the left, to the Market Street side of the gardens.

What kind of crowd is this? What were the categories

devised by Canetti?

Before I can follow the thought there's a loud bang, a shot-gun report, I think, and the crowd bursts apart like shrapnel from the heart of a blast. Some of them rush away in an anti-clockwise whorl like water down a drain, others surge at me and carry me back towards President Street. I am running too, with-out thinking, and then stopping, as the wave subsides and wheels back intuitively towards the sound. We all turn, crouching, or huddled together, or craning boldly as if the whole range of attitudes has been choreographed. I am pinned between two men in front of the hawkers' stalls with the mesh of a gate press-ing against my back.

Tumult on the opposite side of the gardens, men in blue pouring in from both ends of the row of stalls. Riot policemen. Their quarry, the security guards, are also policemen of a kind, but in their berets and boots they look more like soldiers. The front lines clash, men go sprawling over the low walls onto the grass, there are more reports, bouncing back off the office blocks all around, rubber bullets or shotgun pellets, I don't know. But I do know, with every bone and muscle, that I am in the wrong place, I shouldn't be within a day's hike of this madness. I cannot get myself shot in a security guards' strike, especially not with a rubber bullet. No amount of irony could erase the ignominy.

A teargas canister comes arching over the green roofs of the stalls. The frozen moment thaws in an instant into flight. We scramble through a gap in a curving wall, buffeting one another. I plunge out of the stream on the pavement beyond and crouch behind the wall, among hawkers trying to defend spills of oranges and apples, relieved to have brick and mortar between my soft flesh and the guns. My fingers sink into orange pulp on the stone, my feet scatter Quality Street toffees and little build-ing blocks of Chappies bubblegum. All around there is a strange blend of fear and hilarity, faces wincing and laughing. Impossible. I cannot stay here. The sensible thing would be to go east along President, there's a staircase into the parking garage close by. But when I look over my shoulder, the intersection is a blur of men and vehicles and gas – it's drifting downwind! So I must go the other way, crouching behind parked cars, feeling absurdly like a child playing a game. To my right a lane runs through to Pritchard Street, but there are armoured vehicles at the end of that too, beyond the frivolous jet of a fountain, and policemen with helmets, shields and batons.

I peep around the corner of the last stall. The police have taken the plaza, which is almost empty. Three dripping, bedraggled men, scabs the strikers were teaching a lesson about solidarity, are sitting on the edge of the pond with their hands in the air, coughing up water. Blood and slime bearding their chins.

While I'm deciding what to do, a head pops up between the parked cars ahead of me, closer to the library building, and then another. Half a dozen people step gingerly into the open. Innocent bystanders, my kind of people, a pensioner, a middle-aged woman, a couple of schoolchildren. The adults shepherd the youngsters across the plaza and up the stairs. The policemen at the pond glance back idly but do nothing to stop them. A quick knock on the door, which opens to admit them, and they're gone.

I scoot over to the same gap between the cars. From here I have a better view of the plaza and the gardens. Apart from the group at the pond, and a thin cordon of armed men along the periphery, the place is nearly empty. The action has surged away across Simmonds Street and on into the city, leaving behind a trail of litter and placards, jerseys and shoes. I cross the pavement and go up the stairs, hurrying but not running, feeling more and more like a play actor. The stairs are low and wide and it is a long way to the top. I push at the first door but it's locked. Immediately panicky, I hammer on the second one and it opens a crack. Two faces appear, one above the other, a grey-haired librarian and a shaven-headed security guard. Satisfied that I pose no threat, they roll aside a book-laden trolley and let me in.

If I was looking for sanctuary, an oasis of calm and quiet, I've knocked at the wrong door. The lobby looks and sounds like a marketplace. A hubbub as if every unread book had begun to speak at once. Children laughing and talking, acting out their narrow escapes for one another, librarians hurrying upstairs with armfuls of precious papers or manning the barricades, grimly amused or stoical.

'You can't go in there, sir, we've closed the reference section for the safety of the books. But the reading room is open.'

Basil is on duty in the reading room as usual and he fetches the bound issues I'm after. When I tell him what I'm researching, he bursts out laughing, and it suits the unaccustomed uproar. Some men are talking at the windows, watching the drama on the pavement in President Street where the police have their command centre. The air seeping in from outside is still soured with conflict. I find a space at a desk and settle down to work. Later, I'll go upstairs to a window with a view of the gardens and see whether it's safe to leave. If necessary, I'll take the back way out, although I'd rather not. What's the hurry anyway? I can read until it quietens down.

When I lick my finger to turn the page it tastes of orange juice.

Notes and Sources

The main epigraph is from Lionel Abrahams, 'The Fall of van Eck House', an occasional poem about the implosion of this 21-storey sky-scraper in 1983. It appeared in *Journal of a New Man* (Ad Donker, Johannesburg, 1984), pp. 70–72. Escom House, as it was originally known, was built in the mid-thirties for the Electricity Supply Commission and was among the highest reinforced concrete structures of its time. The design was by P. Rogers Cooke and G.E. Pearse & John Fassler. See Clive Chipkin, *Johannesburg Style: Architecture & Society, 1880s–1960s* (David Philip, Cape Town, 1993).

Point A

The epigraph is from Michel de Certeau, *The Practice of Everyday Life* (University of California Press, Berkeley, 1988), p. 108.

2   The Dickens quote is from *A Christmas Carol* (Collins, London, 1932 (1843)), pp. 4–5.

3   M. de Paravicini writes about the closing of the Marymount Nursing Home in 'Toll the last bell', *Sunday Times* Metro, 28 June 1998 (Johannesburg), p. 4. The auction was on 9 July 1998.

5   The avenues were named for Frederick Sleigh Roberts, 1st Earl Roberts of Kandahar; and Horatio Herbert Kitchener, 1st Earl Kitchener of Khartoum.

9   N.I.S.S. stands for National Investigations and Security Systems. The company was bought out by Standby Security in September 2003.

11   Useful facts about the construction of the Carlton Centre, including the details about floor space, are given on public information boards at Level 200. Today the bulk of the city's office and retail space is in Sandton.

      For tips on salesmanship, see F. Bettger, *How I Raised Myself from Failure to Success in Selling* (The World's Work, Kingswood, 1913).

12   The smell of food in the parking garage presumably had to do with the ventilation system, a crucial part of a complex with 50 000 square metres of shopping space entirely underground. Ventilation was a major challenge during the underground construction, and 18 tons of air a minute had to be drawn into the basement for the workers. Strangely enough for a project that made such a strong vertical statement, the early construction must have seemed more like mining than building (public information boards, Level 200).

13   The Sophie Calle exhibition was first shown at the Galerie Arndt, Berlin. And see S. Calle, *The Detachment/Die Entfernung: A Berlin Travel Guide* (Amsterdam, Gordon & Breach, 1999).

15   The sculpture in Pieter Roos Park may be Eduardo Villa's *Reclining figure* (1970) in painted steel. See E. Berman, *Art and Artists of South Africa* (A.A. Balkema, 1983), opposite p. 494.

16   This text draws on reports in various newspapers following the incident on 18 July 1997 and on the remarkable photographs taken by Naashon Zalk. The quote is from the *Star*, 19 July 1997, p. 1. One report (*Star*, 22 July 1997) says that a zoo official rather than a policeman shot the suspect. Max the Gorilla died in May 2004.

19   John Matshikiza also draws the hunter-gatherer analogy in one of his Johannesburg pieces in the *Mail & Guardian*.

21   Towards the end of 2003, the new owner of Eddie's house heightened the garden wall and painted over the mural.

23   The quotes are from the *Star*, 18 November 1999, p. 7.

26   See B. Sachs, *Herman Charles Bosman as I Knew Him* (Golden Era, Johannesburg, 1974). Bosman was a great walker. For an amusing account of the night streets of Johannesburg in the forties, and the difficulties of writing about anything that happens after midnight, see 'Talk of the Town' in *A Cask of Jerepigo* (Dassie Books, Johannesburg, 1957).

32   This took place in the spring of 1991. See R. Bradbury, *Dandelion Wine* (Corgi, London, 1969), pp. 16–18.

33   The eviction occurred in August 1998.

34   The 'long poem of walking' is a phrase used by De Certeau in *The Practice of Everyday Life*, p. 101. The quote about London on a murky winter's night is from *Sketches by Boz* (London, Caxton, 1910 (1836)), p. 244. The quote about the desert region of the night is from *The Uncommercial Traveller* (Everyman, London, 1969 (1860)), p. 135.

37   The universal spanner known as a 'monkey wrench' in English is called a 'Frenchman' in Germany and an 'Englishman' in some other parts of the world. My thanks to Thomas Brückner for this information.

38   The theft occurred towards the end of May 1998.

52   The Canetti quote is from *The Torch in My Ear* (Farrar, Straus & Giroux, New York, 1982), p. 280.

54   The statistics about hijackings are from the *Sunday Times*, 23 May 1999, p. 5; the figures on average earnings of factory workers compared to company directors are from the *Saturday Star*, 11 April 1998, p. 5; the statistics on the number of people employed in the private security industry are from the *Star*, 29 November

1999, p. 8; and the price of the Maranello is from *Car Magazine*, August 1999, pp. 169, 172.

59 The Springbok Boarding House in Van der Walt Street was demolished in the seventies. The Berea Park clubhouse survives as the Graduate Academy of South Africa.

60 Sue Williamson's *Mementoes of District Six* was shown at the Venice Biennale in 1993. See Sue Williamson, *Selected Work* (Double Storey, Cape Town, 2003), pp. 82–3.

61 The comment about the gorilla mask imposed on a woman's face is from the *Sunday Times*, 16 January 2000, p. 14; and the article about the difference between a chimpanzee and a gorilla is in the *Star*, 18 January 2000, p. 1.

62 The comments and quote about laughter are from Elias Canetti, *Crowds and Power* (Victor Gollancz, London, 1962), p. 223.

64 Nigel Henderson, a member of the Independent Group who photographed Bethnal Green between 1949 and 1952, is quoted in Sandra Alvarez de Toledo, 'Street, Wall, Delirium', in *Politics-Poetics documenta X – the book* (Cantz Verlag, Ostfildern, 1997), p. 122.

66 The Hellman quote is from the Quartet edition (London, 1980), p. 3.

67 Canetti's comments are in *The Torch in My Ear*, pp. 354–7.

68 Simon Majola and Themba Nkosi murdered eight men between April 2000 and February 2001, and dumped the bodies in Bruma Lake. In May 2002, Majola was given eight life sentences and Nkosi five.

The man-made lake at the Randburg Waterfront was filled in during 2003. Brightwater Commons, the redesigned centre, features no more than a little brook. Cheryl Adamson, spokesperson for the centre, said, 'Man-made lakes haven't been a raving success in Johannesburg. Although people love being near water, they are not that keen on artificial large expanses of still water.' Property consultant Patrick Flanagan agrees: 'It's very difficult to create an artificial water-cum-leisure environment.' (Nick Wilson, 'Developers are rethinking waterfront projects', *Business Day*, 11 June 2003.)

Yeoville/Hillbrow ridge is a continental watershed: rain that falls to the north of the ridge flows into the Jukskei River and thence to the Indian Ocean, whereas rain that falls to the south flows into the Klip and thence to the Atlantic.

74   Henion Han, *A letter to my cousin in China* (Spookasem, 1999).

78   The De Certeau reference is to the opening of the chapter titled 'Walking in the City', in *The Practice of Everyday Life*, pp.90–93. The phrases from Abrahams are in his poem 'Views and Sites', in *The Writer in Sand* (Ad Donker, Johannesburg, 1988), p. 28.

Point B

The epigraph is from Jorge Luis Borges, 'The South', in *A Personal Anthology* (Grove Press, New York, 1967), p. 18.

80   The facts of the Greeff case are drawn from various reports in the *Star* between 1999 and 2000, and from *Independent Online*, September 2000. Greeff was murdered on Monday 8 November and her body was found on the following Sunday. Justice Jordaan passed sentence on 4 September 2000.

85   *End Bits of Lead* was shown on 'Facts of Life: Contemporary Japanese Art' at the Hayward Gallery in London (October–December 2001). *Autobiography* has not been exhibited.

90   This text draws on various newspaper reports in July 1997. Sandra Laurence describes Fanie Booysen's visit in the *Star*, 22 July 1997, p. 14. The quote about the adoption of Max is from Maxidor's official site: www.maxidor.co.za/max.

92   The quotes are from Elias Canetti, *The Human Province* (Seabury Press, New York, 1978), pp. 98, 26, 197, 185.

93   *Leaping Impala* was subsequently restored at the Renzo Vignali Artistic Foundry and reinstalled outside Anglo American's Main Street headquarters in May 2002.

       The AbdouMaliq Simone quote is from his essay 'Globalization and the identity of African urban practices', in Hilton Judin and Ivan Vladislavić (eds), *blank_Architecture, apartheid and after* (NAi Publishers, Rotterdam, 1998), D8, p. 186.

97   The comment on Dickens and the noisy rhythms of London is from Walter Benjamin's *Passagenwerk*.

99   N.I.S.S.: National Investigations and Security Systems.

103   Isaac Mofokeng died in the Weskoppies psychiatric hospital in November 2005.

107   This text draws on reports in the *Star* on 13 and 14 September 2000.

111   The Takis Xenopoulos story is from the *Star* Tonight, 31 July 2001, p. 8.

114   The garden-gate telephone service proliferated during 2000 (the one attached to the row houses in Nourse Street appeared in November).

115   The back door has since become a permanent arrangement and is formally signposted.

116   For a description of Martin Kippenberger's *Metro-Net* see Roberto Ohrt et al, *The Last Stop West* (MAK Center, Los Angeles, 1998); or *Politics-Poetics documenta X – the book* (Cantz Verlag, Ostfildern, 1997).

120 The Woody Guthrie quote about painting is from *Bound for Glory* (E.P. Dutton & Co., New York, 1943), p. 316.

121 See Eric Itzkin, *Gandhi's Johannesburg* (Wits University Press, Johannesburg, 2000).

123 I have not found a definitive account of where Akasegawa got the name, but the story goes that he borrowed it from an American baseball player. This legendary player, the most expensive purchase ever in the Japanese league, caused a huge stir when he arrived in the country, but suffered a preseason injury and never started a game. He is sometimes given as Gary Leah Thomasson, who was signed by the Yomiuri Giants in the early eighties, although the identification seems doubtful as this player had a good batting average (according to the baseball sites).

124 Henion Han, *A letter to my cousin in China* (Spookasem, 1999).

125 The gate extension is at 20 Albemarle Street.

126 A semi in Eleanor Street (22/22a) has the same gable rash as the house at 3 Broadway.

127 The quoted phrase is from William Kentridge.

128 The HIV/AIDS sign in Troyeville was part of a collaborative project between artist Sue Williamson and people living with Aids. This particular sign was made by John Masuku in 2002. The message was photographed and paired with a portrait of Masuku in Williamson's *From the Inside* series. 'The willingness to be named is important in a society where shame and silence over the illness prevail.' Sue Williamson, *Selected Work* (Double Storey, Cape Town, 2003), Artist's notes, p. 28.

132 This mural was designed by Ilse Pahl. In another account of Webster's murder he has just come back from walking the dogs, and in yet another he has been to the bakery and has a loaf of fresh bread under his arm.

133   There are memorable accounts of Johannesburg life everywhere in Bosman's work. This text specifically acknowledges 'Talk of the Town', 'Street Processions' and 'The Recognizing Blues'. One of Bosman's most interesting pieces on the city, simply titled 'Johannesburg', was republished in *A Cask of Jerepigo*. The quotation from Abrahams is in 'Mr Bosman: A Protégé's Memoir of Herman Charles Bosman' (typescript). When Abrahams visited Bosman at his office in High Court Buildings in the mid-forties, he was charmed by the fact that the doormat was embossed with 'HCB' – Bosman's initials.

Today, High Court Buildings faces onto Gandhi Square (rededicated in 2003). Close by there is a statue of Gandhi dressed for court, the hem of his robe lifted by the wind. If you wish to see how well a statue of Bosman would suit the balcony of his old office, the statue of Gandhi looking down from his pedestal has exactly the right attitude and can be transposed to the second-floor nook at a glance.

Lionel Abrahams's poem 'Place' carries the note 'A party of white Johannesburgers reads Zbigniew Herbert, Holub and other poets near a mine dump, Summer 1969'. See *Journal of a New Man* (Ad Donker, Johannesburg, 1984).

Hillary Hamburger describes her first view of Abrahams at a Roberts Avenue tram stop in the introduction to 'Reality is the Richest Source: An Interview with a Friend', in Graeme Friedman and Roy Blumenthal (eds), *A Writer in Stone: South African Writers Celebrate the 70th Birthday of Lionel Abrahams* (David Philip, Cape Town, 1998).

Also see Louise Masreliez, 'Representing the Subjective: Private Niche and Home – A Subjective Approach to Architecture', *Nordic Journal of Architectural Research*, 1–2: 83–91 (1998). Thanks to Stefan Helgesson for drawing my attention to this.

136   The story about the emperor Yang-Ti is told in Victor Segalen, *Paintings*, translated and introduced by Andrew Harvey and Iain Watson, Quartet Encounters series (Quartet, London, 1991), pp. 138–41. The quote is from p. 141.

137   See *Business Report*, 11 November 2002, p. 11.

138 SADF: South African Defence Force. Ernest Ullman's monu-
mental sculptures have made him a favourite of Johannesburg's
scavengers, who value their art by the kilogram. His *Family Group*
was stolen from outside the public library in September 2003.

Itineraries

This index traces the order of the previously published cycles and suggests some other thematic pathways through the book.

The routes are classified as follows:

L = Long
M = Moderate
S = Short

An accidental island (L)
4, 5, 10, 17, 20, 21, 22, 27, 31, 39, 40, 43, 45, 48, 51, 57, 66, 67, 69, 76
This cycle was first published in *fifty-one years: David Goldblatt*, edited by David Goldblatt with Corinne Diserens and Okwui Enwezor (Museu d'Art Contemporani de Barcelona & Actar, Barcelona, 2001). An abbreviated version appeared in French translation in *meet* no. 9, *São Paulo/Le Cap* (La Maison des Écrivains Étrangers et des Traducteurs de Saint-Nazaire, 2005).

Artists' book (M)
10   Esther Mahlangu,
13   Sophie Calle,
29   Jeff Lok,
40   Mahlangu,
50   Ilona Anderson,
53   Renier le Roux,
60   Sue Williamson,

Beggars and sellers (M)
4, 11, 17, 45, 52, 73, 86, 91, 98, 104, 105, 110, 113, 114, 134

Body language (M)
4, 8, 17, 23, 24, 41, 50, 61, 62, 63, 67, 86, 101, 137

Branko (M)
3, 8, 12, 22, 29, 40, 46, 91, 97, 117, 118

City centre (L)
115, 116, 117, 118, 120, 121, 122, 123, 125, 126, 127, 128, 130, 131, 132, 133, 135, 136, 137, 138
This cycle was first published in *Overseas,* a book of photographs by Roger Palmer (Edition Fotohof, Salzburg, 2004).

Closer together (M)
21, 25, 27, 31, 42, 52, 71, 74, 76, 77, 92, 119, 124, 126

Engaging the Gorilla (L)
7, 16, 19, 23, 24, 35, 36, 37, 46, 47, 52, 53, 54, 55, 58, 61, 62, 72
A short version of this cycle was first published in German translation under the title 'Die Lebensweise des Gorillas' in *Helfershelfer: Türbremse, Tropfenfänger und andere obligate Symbionten*, edited by Jörg Adam, Dominik Harborth & Andrea Vilter (Edition Solitude & Grafisches Zentrum Drucktechnik, Stuttgart/Ditzingen, 2000). The piece appeared again as 'The habits of the Gorilla' in the English version of the book, *Second Aid: Doorstops, drip-catchers and other symbiotic gadgets* (avedition, Ludwigsburg, 2003).

Falling see Walking

Gardens (S)
19, 21, 48, 84, 90, 100, 102, 122, 125
Ghosting through (S)
39, 42, 66, 75, 106, 107, 119, 127, 131, 133, 135, 137

Home territory (L)
2, 48, 51, 74, 76, 78, 79, 89, 100, 105, 108, 119, 127, 134, 136

Insecurity see Security

Liars and thieves (L)
13, 16, 19, 23, 32, 38, 46, 47, 52, 54, 57, 59, 80, 91, 93, 94, 96, 97, 103

Memorials (M)
6, 15, 29, 30, 44, 50, 51, 60, 85, 111, 121, 122, 132, 133

Object lessons (L)
27, 29, 30, 32, 33, 35, 36, 37, 53, 56, 57, 58, 59, 60, 64, 65, 82, 85, 94, 101, 106, 112, 113, 123, 126

Old lives (S)
3, 21, 48, 59, 74, 81, 82, 86, 109, 112, 124, 129, 130

Painted walls (S) also see Walls
10, 21, 22, 40, 43, 66, 106, 120, 128, 132, 136

Safe and sound (L)
79, 80, 83, 84, 87, 88, 89, 90, 94, 95, 96, 97, 99, 101, 102, 103, 106, 52, 107, 110, 111
A short version of this cycle was first published in *Connect 4: The Wall* (Arts International, New York, 2002) under the title 'Portrait with keys'. An even briefer sequence appeared in Portuguese translation as 'Retrato com chaves', in *Valor* (São Paulo, 10–12 May 2002), a special edition produced for the São Paulo Biennale; and in Spanish translation as 'Retrato con llaves', in the catalogue *Moulène/Sala São Paulo 2002*, Tunnel Vision (Images En Manœuvres Éditions/Carta Blanca éditions, Marseille, 2002).

Security (L)

1, 12, 13, 20, 35, 41, 52, 55, 72, 75, 83, 87, 88, 95, 115, 125, 131, 138

Self storage (L)

28, 41, 42, 44, 49, 50, 56, 59, 60, 63, 64, 65, 68, 70, 71, 73, 74, 75, 77, 78
This cycle has not been published before.

Street addresses, Johannesburg (L)

1, 2, 3, 6, 8, 9, 11, 12, 13, 14, 15, 18, 25, 26, 29, 30, 32, 33, 34, 38
This cycle was first published in *blank_Architecture, apartheid and after*, edited by Hilton Judin and Ivan Vladislavić (Netherlands Architecture Institute, Rotterdam, 1998).

Trade secrets (L)

81, 82, 85, 86, 91, 92, 93, 98, 100, 104, 105, 108, 109, 112, 113, 114, 119, 124, 129, 134
This cycle has not been published before.

Underground (S)

12, 31, 39, 108, 115, 116, 137, 138

Walking (L)

2, 4, 5, 14, 15, 17, 28, 32, 34, 57, 62, 64, 67, 69, 89, 99, 105, 119, 123, 127, 130, 133

Walls (S) also see Painted walls

1, 14, 24, 29, 57, 94, 131

Water (S)

5, 28, 68, 69, 87, 108, 129

Writers' book (M)

2   Charles Dickens,
26   Herman Charles Bosman,
32   Ray Bradbury,
34   Dickens,
49   Louis Fehler,
62   Elias Canetti,

Young lives (M)

Author's Note

As a student at Wits in the seventies, I chanced upon a guided tour led by a young social historian called Tim Couzens. There was nothing formal about it. A few of us just piled into a kombi and drove around Joburg while Tim told stories – about the Doornfontein yards, Vrededorp, Langlaagte, the American Board Mission School, the Bantu Men's Social Centre, Hindu temples, mine compounds, lunatic asylums, and other remarkable things he would later put into *The New African*. It was a revelation. In a single afternoon, a Johannesburg concealed within the place familiar to me came to the surface, like one of Calvino's invisible cities, which are magical because they are real – Olinda, always renewing itself, or Raissa, the unhappy city ignorant of the happy city at its heart, or Berenice, the unjust and the just city, wrapped in one another like onion skins.

Some twenty years later, Graeme Friedman and Roy Blumenthal invited me to contribute to a collection celebrating the 70th birthday of Lionel Abrahams (published as *A Writer in Stone*). Soon enough, I was caught up in rereading the poems, essays and polemics of Abrahams, another teacher who had become my friend. One of the things that struck me was how intensely his work grappled with what it means to be a citizen of Johannesburg, and inspired by his example I made the first notes towards a book on the city. His poem 'The Fall of van Eck House' was a touchstone. I am sorry Lionel did not live to see my book published.

The writing really began in 1998, when I co-edited *blank_Architecture, apartheid and after* with Hilton Judin. Having to produce my own contribution for the book felt like a burden at the time, but I am glad now that Hilton would not take no for an answer. The sequence of short texts called 'Street addresses, Johannesburg' formed the basis for everything else.

The next year I took up a fellowship at Akademie Schloss Solitude in Stuttgart. 'Street addresses' had uncovered themes worth exploring and the fellowship allowed me to do so. A large part of this book was drafted there. I am grateful to the institution, its director Jean-Baptiste Joly and its literary juror J.M. Coetzee for giving me the opportunity.

Many of the texts have been published as cycles in other contexts. I would not have dealt with the material this way had various writers and artists not asked me to contribute to projects of their own. Such commissions not only shaped the concerns of the book but gave me the means to go on with it in a suitably roundabout way.

Corinne Diserens set the pattern by inviting me to write for the catalogue of a retrospective exhibition of David Goldblatt's photographs, which she was curating with Okwui Enwezor. David kindly gave me access to his archives while I was writing 'An accidental island'. Mela Dávila at the Museum of Contemporary Art in Barcelona (MACBA) coordinated the publication of *fifty-one years: David Goldblatt*.

The circular structure of 'An accidental island' owes something to the work of the Austrian architect Klaus Metzler, whom I got to know in Germany. Klaus was undertaking a walking tour around the peripheries of Stuttgart, following the old and now largely forgotten city borderline and documenting the route in words and photographs. His project has subsequently been published as *Blinde Grenzen: ein architektonisches Grenzprojekt links um Stuttgart* (Edition Solitude, Stuttgart, 2000).

'Portrait with keys', the third cycle and the one that eventually lent its title to the book, was prepared for Radhika Subramaniam and Rosalind C. Morris at *Connect* and published in 2002. Extracts also appeared in Spanish and Portuguese in publications linked to the São Paulo Biennale, and for this I must thank Jean-Charles Massera, along with Jean-Luc Moulène and Anri Sala.

Roger Palmer commissioned 'City centre' for his book of photographs *Overseas*, which accompanied a retrospective exhibition of his work at Salzburg's Galerie Fotohof in 2004. I am grateful to Roger for making me part of his book, and to Rainer Iglar and Michael Mauracher at Edition Fotohof for publishing it.

In 1999, I contributed an essay on the steering lock to *Helfershelfer* by Jörg Adam, Dominik Harborth and Andrea Vilter. This German publication accompanied a design exhibition devoted to 'symbiotic gadgets', secondary inventions that depend for their use on other objects (the analogy with my own method is clear enough). The English translation, *Second Aid*, appeared at the end of 2003. It was only then that I fully appreciated the affinity between 'The habits of the Gorilla' and *Portrait with Keys*, and decided to incorporate the essay into the book.

The various cycles were finally interleaved to create a single sequence. The paths of the original cycles and some other patterns are traced in the Itineraries. My model for this thematic index is in Humphrey Jennings's great compendium of readings, *Pandemonium: The Coming of the Machine as Seen by Contemporary Observers*. Apart from a few updates in the notes, my texts have not been revised to reflect changes that may have happened since they were drafted.

Many editors have helped me to refine the work. In addition to those mentioned above, I thank Matt Weiland for his astute editing of extracts for *Granta*, which gave me pointers for improving the whole book. My agent Isobel Dixon read various versions of the manuscript and gave me good advice about it. I am also indebted to Tony Morphet and William Dicey for their very helpful comments.

The 'Visitors' book' (as it would have been indexed in the Itineraries) was my scheme to invite some of the people mentioned in this book into its pages as a sympathetic or argumentative chorus. I am grateful to my friends for arriving with so much enthusiasm and departing with such good grace. My intention was to make the book theirs, which of course it still is. They are Alan Schlesinger, Chas Unwin, Dave Edwards, Glynis O'Hara, Lesley Lawson, Mark Gevisser, Mike Kirkwood and Sean Fourie.

And then there is Minky, always at the heart of my book and the life going on around it.

Ivan Vladislavić
February 2006

© Cato Lein

Born in Pretoria in 1957, Ivan Vladislavić has lived in Johannesburg since 1977. He is the author of five works of fiction and has been awarded the Olive Schreiner Prize and the South African *Sunday Times* fiction prize. *Portrait with Keys* was shortlisted for the Ondaatje Prize and won the Alan Paton Prize, South Africa's major nonfiction award.